Not My Will but Thine

An Autobiography

Judie Brown

American Life League
P.O. Box 1350, Stafford, VA 22555

Brown, Judie
Not My Will but Thine: An Autobiography
ISBN 1-890712-31-0

Cover design by Bonnie Seers

Printed in the United States of America.

Dedication

I have often heard it said that behind every good man is a good woman—and vice versa. In my case that is truer than anyone will ever know. This autobiography is being prepared just prior to the 34th wedding anniversary of Mr. and Mrs. Paul Anthony Brown. Our trials have been many, our joys have been extraordinary, and our family continues to grow in grace, love and, of course, grandchildren.

And so I dedicate this book to my husband, Paul, without whom I could never have done so much of what God has called me to do. Paul Brown is my hero. He is my conscience. He is the source of my sanity. He is my counselor. Yes, sometimes he is difficult and stubborn—and so am I. But as the song goes, he is the wind beneath my wings.

I love you, dear.

Table of

Contents

Prologue

It is not in my nature to write about myself. I believe sincerely that I am nothing more than God's servant and that I could accomplish nothing apart from His grace. I learned from the late Father John Hardon, S. J., that total surrender means delivering into Christ's hands everything including my liberty, my understanding, my memory and my will. There is really no story about me, but a story about a human being who has tried very hard to be whatever the Lord asked me to be. Often I have failed; often I have sorrowed over my sinful nature; but more often have I praised Him for loving me and having patience with me.

I am aware that each of us, as children of God, has a special mission in life, and that periodically most of us need to be refreshed in our awareness of that awesome truth. So I offer this account of my continuing pilgrimage in the hope that you may see—even in a life as ordinary as my own—that there is no person whose experiences are without purpose in God's plan. If we will allow the Lord to work through us, tremendous things can happen. Each day is a promise from God that life need never be wasted. As Archbishop Fulton Sheen has said, time is so very precious that God only gives it to us one second at a time.

Walk with me through the past 58 years. Laugh with me, cry with me, celebrate with me, and mourn with me. See, if you will, the mystery of faith that continues to propel me even now: often beyond my understanding, sometimes even against my will, but always with the trust that in God everything has a purpose.

I am not suggesting that my life is a road map or model for others to follow. It surely is not. It is, however, a story of a woman who has come to know the value of faith and who has seen the Lord work because of it.

In the Gospel of John we learn of our union with Christ and how it comes about. We learn, too, that if we are open to the Lord's will in our lives, we soon understand how it is that He has chosen each one of us to be a part of His plan for all mankind.

> *You are my friends if you do the things I command you. No longer do I call you servants, because the servant does not know what his master does. But I have called you friends, because all things that I have heard from my Father I have made known to you. You have not chosen me; it is I who have chosen you.*
>
> *—John 15:14–16*

Chapter One

A Mother's Love: No Matter What

~

1944–1950

In him who is the source of my strength, I have strength for everything.
—*Philippians 4:13*

As my mother never tired of pointing out, I entered the world a difficult and obstinate person. I was a "breech" baby, meaning that I tried to come out of the birth canal backwards. The doctors had to turn me around before I could be born. Even while I was still in the womb, I was giving others a challenge. Some things, my mother would say, never change.

This was in March 1944. My mother had been married to my father for a little longer than a year. My sister Sheila was born only 18 months later. Though I was too young to remember it, it was then that my life changed radically.

While my mother was still in Our Lady of Angels Hospital in Los Angeles recovering from Sheila's birth, my father deserted us. Within a week of Sheila's birth, he was gone from our lives forever.

As it turned out, my mother had been his fifth wife—a fact she never knew.

The pain was intense at the time my father left. Mama's selfless love had been betrayed. Now she was left with two small babies and nowhere to go.

Right:
Bertha Tekla Shreck,
my maternal
grandmother, at
her wedding to
Louis W. Baldi;
Harry and Elsie Baldi
are behind them.

In later years my grandmother—Mama's mother, Bertha Tekla Baldi—told me how worried she was about my mother during this time. For months after the divorce Mama wept in anguish. She never let my sister or me see that side of her, though—she suffered in private. It was almost a year before she was able to start putting her life, and ours, back together again.

Ultimately we moved in with Grandma and Grandpa Baldi. They opened their hearts, and their modest home on Harcourt Avenue in Los Angeles, to the three of us. They made life as joyful for Mama as they could, always realizing that her dreams of home and family might be dashed forever.

How well I remember those years. Mama would leave for work each morning, leaving Sheila and me under the care of our doting grandparents. Grandpa worked as a bricklayer—when work could be found. When there was none, he stayed home and helped look after my sister and me. He played with us and talked with us, smoking his cigar and blowing big smoke rings in the air. He was cheerful and playful—until we did something to make Grandma upset. Then he got more than a little irritated with us.

Below: Me at four months.

Far Right: Grandma Baldi in 1951.

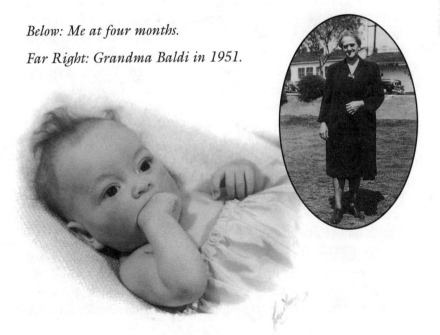

Grandma and Grandpa, like all good Germans, believed in orderliness and obedience. The rules they set for us, and the standards of behavior to which they held us, were unbending. That doesn't mean that Sheila and I were especially orderly or obedient, however. We knew there would be consequences when we crossed the line. But we never let that stop us from crossing it anyway.

For example, Grandpa did not want us to take food to our room. But Sheila and I had other ideas and became very adept at crawling under the bed covers with cookies, milk, candy, chips and other goodies we had smuggled out of the kitchen. Of course there was always incriminating evidence—crumbs, spills and wrappers that we had left behind. But even being caught and punished didn't seem to spoil our desire to do it again the next night.

Not all my childhood experiences had to do with being naughty, though. I especially remember Wednesday nights, when I would go with Grandma to the weekly Rosary. We'd leave the house right after dinner and walk around the corner to the home of a neighbor lady. In her living room were a vigil candle and a beautiful statue of Our Lady crushing the head of the serpent. I remember kneeling next to Grandma on the hard floor—how it must have pained her aging knees—and being perfectly content to pray the entire Rosary. As we walked home I would ask why we couldn't go more often. I remember the smile on my mother's face when we got home. She could see that praying with Grandma was something I really loved to do.

Grandma and Grandpa loved us and were only too happy to do things to please us. Sheila and I quickly learned to exploit their generous natures. Whenever the ice cream man came down our street, we could always rely on one or the other (or both) of them to treat us to a Popsicle. Sometimes we were able to orchestrate three or four treats in a single day. Needless to say, we both developed weight problems at an early age.

By the time I entered first grade at St. John's school, I was accomplished at manipulating others to get what I wanted. If I wanted to go home early, I told the teacher I was sick. If I wanted attention, I claimed to be having an asthma attack. If I complained loudly enough and long enough, I always got my way. Except for the asthma attacks—some of which were quite real—Sheila could play all the same cards.

I shudder to think what sort of children we would have become had it not been for the man who entered Mama's life.

Chapter Two

A Father for All Seasons

∼

1951–1957

Husbands should love their wives as they do their own bodies. He who loves his wife loves himself. Observe that no one ever hates his own flesh; no, he nourishes it and takes care of it as Christ cares for the church—for we are members of his body.
—Ephesians 5:28–29

Mama was still young, and quite attractive, and she had two younger brothers who were always bringing someone home to meet her. I remember some of those fellows, and—to be quite frank—I'm thankful Mama had the good taste to pass on them.

All but one, that is.

Chester Limbourne came to know my mother through Uncle George, Mama's baby brother. I remember the first time Chester came to the house. I remember him coming many other times, to take Mama out for the evening. And I especially remember the night Mama talked to Grandma about getting married again—or, at first, about not getting married again.

Our mother's marital status was a topic of great interest to Sheila and me, so we had our ears pressed to the door as Mama explained to Grandma why she felt she could not accept Chester Limbourne's proposal of marriage—even though she thought him the most wonderful man in the world.

Mama was 34 at the time, and she suffered from rheumatoid arthritis in her legs and arms. She had to go to downtown Los Angeles for "gold treatments" at City of Hope Hospital on a regular basis. She was afraid that her arthritis, combined with the fact that she had two children, would simply be too much for Chester for handle.

Sheila and I were horrified. We didn't know much about the world at that age, but we thought Chester Limbourne was terrific. He always gave us a big hug when he came for Mama, and he was so nice to Grandma and Grandpa. We were happy to see Mama with someone who was so nice, and we couldn't believe she'd pass up an opportunity to marry him.

Chester finally passed over all Mama's objections by focusing on the one thing that made marriage the right decision for her. He simply loved her more than anything else in the world, and he wanted more than anything to be her husband and our father.

From the moment they walked down the aisle, Sheila and I knew that we had a real father, someone who loved our mother and us, someone who cared about the security of our little family. Though we were not bone of his bone and flesh of his flesh, he always treated us as though we were. The sacrifices he made for us would require another book to recount.

And so, in 1951, we moved into a house of our own. Sheila and I had never seen Mama so happy. We almost didn't know what to make of it. But we never questioned that life was wonderful.

~

Our little family was soon blessed by two additions. A brother, Mark, was born in 1952. Two years later my sister Ann arrived. The babies were the center of attention. I loved taking care of them for my mother, who was still bothered by her arthritis.

Mark required special care, because he was born with Down syndrome. He seldom cried; in fact it seemed as though he always had a smile on his face, and whenever he became ill, Mama became very anxious—and with good reason.

Mark's immune system was underdeveloped, which meant that even the slightest sniffle could swiftly develop into pneumonia. We all did our best to protect him from germs, but from time to time he would catch cold and have to be nursed around the clock. When that happened, Mama, Sheila and I had to team up. Mama would handle the night shift, and Sheila and I would take turns staying home from school so we could care for Mark during the day while Mama slept.

In the fall of 1954, when he was two and a half years old, Mark came down with one of his occasional colds. But this time was different. He was gravely ill. He didn't respond to being touched. He was in a state of sleepiness from which he never seemed to awaken completely.

I came home from school one afternoon to find Mama in a panic. She was on the phone with the doctor. Before I knew it we were out the door, in the car, racing to the hospital. I sat next to Mama in the front seat, holding Mark in my lap. He was so weak he was barely breathing. It was a 15-minute ride to the hospital. Mark didn't make it. He died in my arms.

I'll never forget that awful afternoon. Daddy met us at the hospital. So did the doctor, who coldly pronounced Mark dead and then had the gall to tell us that we were all "probably better off."

Looking back, I'm sure my mother always knew that Mark's condition was such that he could not survive to adulthood. But her faith enabled her to use each moment she spent caring for him as a testimony to her confidence that God would look after her son. She and Daddy always treated Mark and Ann as though they were equal, even though Mark was never able to walk or even crawl. We used to sit together on Sunday evenings and watch the Walt Disney program. We all enjoyed it, but Mark enjoyed it more than anyone. Just hearing the theme song made him giggle and bounce up and down. Indeed, all music affected him that way—it made him happy.

We went through the next few days after Mark's death as if in a trance. Friends and family members flocked to our aid. Though each one offered loving sympathy, the loss was simply too much for my mother to bear. Against all reason, she blamed herself for what had happened. Wanting to be alone in her grief, she shut out everyone except Daddy—who was, as always, her rock, her fortress, her friend.

~

Things only got tougher for Mama as the year went on. Her arthritis hit her harder than ever. She developed bleeding ulcers. She was hospitalized a couple of times. With each setback,

Above: My mother upon her engagement to Chester Limbourne in 1952.

Right: My parents on their wedding day.

Daddy grew stronger, more compassionate, more in love with this woman who was suffering so.

He also grew more demanding of the rest of us, to be patient with Mama, to love her, to avoid doing things that would upset her. Of course, all children hear their fathers scold them, "Don't upset your mother." But I always felt that Daddy spoke more from a genuine concern for her well-being than from a simple desire to keep us in line. He loved her so much that he suffered with her, though he never suggested that her difficulties were weighing him down.

I still remember the small but beautifully decorated Christmas tree we placed at Mark's grave the year he died. I also remember Mama's tears as we placed the tree by his grave marker. It became an annual trip for us, and each time we felt the loss as keenly as though Mark had just left us the day before.

I see now that the aftermath of Mark's death was so severe because of the unselfish love my parents had for him. Had they cared less about him while he was alive, they would have cared less about his death. But from the moment he was born, when

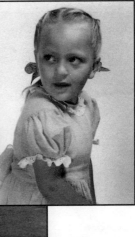

Right: Me in 1954.

Below: Mama and Daddy at Mark's grave.

they rejected the doctor's suggestion that they put Mark in a home somewhere because he could never lead a "normal" life, my parents loved Mark as deeply as they loved all the rest of us.

Maybe it is fair to say they loved him even more, because his needs were so much greater. He required long, hard hours of care, which they surely would rather have spent doing something else; but they never neglected him. He needed to be at home virtually all the time, which many would find inconvenient; but they never complained. There was simply nothing they would not have done for their son, while also making sure that my sisters and I never felt left out.

Looking back on this hectic period, I cannot help but wonder how Daddy coped with the powerful emotions that must have welled up inside him. Mama's rapid deterioration meant he never really had time to mourn the death of his only son. I wonder how many other men would have handled it the way he did, always placing his wife's needs first? I was too young to appreciate what he was going through, or the grace with which he handled it.

No words can do justice to his role in our family through those dark days. Is it any wonder that I consider Chester Limbourne a great man?

Chapter Three

Going to K-Mart

1958–1964

*I will instruct you and show you the way
you should walk; I will counsel you, keeping my eye on you.*

—Psalm 32:8

Gradually life began to level out. Ann, the baby of the family, turned three. I turned 13—a very large 13, I might add. I was seriously overweight. Had I been a boy, I'm sure I could have been a star lineman on the high school football team.

Mama's arthritis seemed to recede a bit. She moved a bit slower than she would have liked, but she managed to do pretty much everything she wanted to do. And she had a lot of things she wanted to do. She served as chauffeur for the nuns at our local grade school and as head chef for the big weekly dinners we held at our house for all the family—as many as 20 people each week. She prepared baked goods for the church whenever she was asked, made most of our clothes, and even held down a part-time job stuffing envelopes and collating materials for a local business. She never complained, never made excuses, never asked for sympathy. She just did what she felt she should do and made the best of her physical limitations.

Somehow, in spite of all this, she still had the ability to be there for us when we needed her. She seemed to radiate love to others. My sisters and I never brought home a "stranger." Everyone was welcome; everyone was made to feel part of the family. In fact, countless friends came home with us after school, or dropped in on weekends, just to talk with Mrs. Limbourne, the wonderful lady who always had time to listen, a good word to say, and a warm smile with brown eyes that could cut right through your troubles.

We were just an ordinary family, dealing with the problems that everyone faced in the late 1950s. When I turned 16, Daddy decided to take on the job of teaching me to drive. We went to the Hollywood Race Track in suburban Inglewood, which had a huge parking lot. Daddy figured I'd need plenty of room if I were to avoid endangering the safety of others. And he was right. To this day I cannot parallel park. I even have trouble backing up.

It was also about this time that I decided to begin a chapter of the Johnny Mathis Fan Club. I answered an ad in a teen magazine from someone in Maine who was looking for help expanding the club. I wrote tons of letters and made hundreds of long-distance phone calls. I finally found myself president of the largest chapter of the entire fan club. I wrote regularly to Johnny

Mathis, whom I adored but had never met. I recounted all the details of how the fan club was growing, trusting that he pored over every word I wrote.

Then one day the phone rang. It was Johnny Mathis' agent. Johnny was going to be making an appearance soon at the Coconut Grove and wanted to invite my parents and me to come as his personal guests. After the show, we were invited backstage to meet Johnny in his dressing room. I was in heaven.

I marvel at my parents' patience through all this. They never told me I was being a silly teenage girl, never even complained about the cost of all those letters and phone calls. They just supported me in what I wanted to do, believing that children were better served if they had wholesome activities that helped them understand the ways of the world.

They sacrificed for us in so many ways—music lessons twice a week for 10 years, new clothes when we simply "had to have them," an excellent (and expensive) education at the parish school. When I think of the many things they did without, I'm saddened by the fact that as a child I never appreciated, let alone thanked them for, all that they did for me. If anything, I only grew more demanding, and more outspoken when I didn't get my way. It took me a long time to learn what Daddy so often told me—"Money doesn't grow on trees, Judie."

But I began to learn the value of a dollar when I started taking various part-time jobs. I delivered Fuller Brush products for a local salesman. I taught beginning accordion at the studio where I took lessons. I filled in behind the jewelry counter of the nearby Kresge's five-and-dime. None of these jobs demanded a great deal of time, but they did begin to teach me the importance of commitment and hard work.

I also volunteered as a "candy striper," or nurse's aide, at the local hospital. I was easily bored, and needed lots of activities to keep me busy. Working in the hospital didn't bring in any money, but it taught me some important lessons. It cemented a lesson I had learned from the way we had cared for Mark: those who are suffering are the ones for whom we must make time. I still remember the faces of patients who would see me and know that I would always stop and talk with them for a while, even if they were not going to buy one of my candy bars or packages of Kleenex. My grandfather lived right across the street from the hospital—he had moved there after Grandma died—and I would visit him, too, cleaning up the apartment or just chatting.

~

As high school graduation approached, the time came to set-tle on some plans for the future. I knew I wanted to go to col-lege, and at first I thought I wanted to be a child psychologist. I had good grades and I was even offered a full scholarship to New York University. But I turned it down because I realized my career goals were too uncertain for me to leave my family and go 3,000 miles away. My parents were thrilled by the scholarship offer—and relieved, I think, when I decided not to accept it.

I weighed all my options and discussed things at length with my parents. We talked a lot about the medical profession, with which I was so enamored. Mama was afraid that my inclination to become personally involved with anyone who had a problem might be my undoing. I had to agree.

We finally determined that the business world provided the best fit. So I stayed at home, stayed on at the local Kresge's as a bookkeeper and registered for the fall semester at a local college.

A year later I decided it was time to move out and live on my own. I took an apartment just a few blocks from my parents' house. Not long after, my father made a decision he had been contemplating for some time. The family would move away. My baby sister, Ann, was now eight years old, and Daddy wanted her to have a horse and a big yard and the kind of environment that southern California could no longer provide. And so, in the summer of 1963, Mama and Daddy and Sheila and Ann packed up and moved to Oregon, while I remained in Los Angeles.

My career was developing nicely. Within a year I had been promoted from the local store to the western regional headquar-ters of what was now known as the K-Mart Corporation. I con-tinued my studies, worked under a couple of brilliant corporate vice presidents, and within a year was invited to become the western regional office manager—a position that had never before been offered to anyone younger than 30.

After consulting my family, I accepted the promotion. It meant a lot of travel, and discontinuing my education, but it seemed like the right step. I began crisscrossing the 11 states in K-Mart's western region, overseeing training for new stores and meeting people who were in upper-level management positions with the company.

One of these was a very interesting man named Paul Brown.

Chapter Four

Romancing the Blarney Stone

~

1964–1967

*Love never fails. There are in the end
three things that last: faith, hope and love,
and the greatest of these is love.*
                                    —*1 Corinthians 13:13*

Traveling around the western United States in the early 1960s was a great job for a young woman. I had freedom, I had a good salary, and I had executive responsibilities and the perks that went with them.

Frankly, it has always been a bit hard for me to understand why some women complain about the difficulties of competing in the job world. I can honestly say I never faced any sort of discrimination. I worked hard, I did my job well, and I was recognized and rewarded for it. What has changed since those days? Has the business world suddenly turned against talent and hard work? Or are women trying to imitate or replace men, rather than complement and support them? In any case, my own corporate adventure was wonderful.

One of my first assignments, in the fall of 1964, was to help open a new store in Ogden, Utah. This particular store had special importance to the company: it was going to pioneer a new design. An experienced manager, Paul Brown, had been assigned to oversee the opening and to make sure that the layout of the store was perfect, right down to the last tube of toothpaste.

Mr. Brown, I was told, was bright, energetic and experienced. There was just one problem. For some reason, he absolutely refused to punch in and out on his time card, yet he insisted on being paid overtime. Since part of my job was to serve as supervisor of payroll, one of my first tasks was to set Mr. Brown straight.

I went looking for him one Thursday afternoon as my staff was trying to complete the week's payroll. I found him squatting down in front of a display case, arranging merchandise on the bottom shelf.

"Mr. Brown?" I asked.

He didn't even look up. "Yeah," he muttered.

"Mr. Paul A. Brown?" I asked, using my most intimidating supervisory tone of voice.

Now he looked up. "What do you want?" he snapped.

"It's about your overtime," I said. "You haven't been punching in your time card, and I can't pay you until you do."

"Go to h—."

I stood over him, all 210 pounds of me, and gave him a stern lecture on K-Mart company policy. The company would not allow me to pay his overtime, I said, if he did not record the hours. The company was most generous with managers, I said, but the company also needed a record, and so on.

He didn't say anything. He just stood up, glared at me for a second, then shook his head and walked away. As far as I know, he never did punch a time card—he probably felt it was too demeaning for a manager—and he never got paid for his overtime.

I, of course, was speechless with anger. Nobody was going to talk to Judie Limbourne like that. For the next three years, whenever our paths crossed, I always found some way to insert a snide remark or otherwise express my dislike for him.

So you can imagine my reaction when a friend suggested, some three years later, that I call a halt to the feud. It was embarrassing to the company, she said, and it couldn't possibly be doing my career any good. Besides, she said, Paul Brown was really a warm, friendly person, and she was sure I'd like him if I would only give him a chance.

Well, why not? It had been three years, after all. A lot of water had flowed under the bridge. I had advanced in position and salary. I had lost 80 pounds. The store he now managed was only an hour's drive away, in Bellevue, Washington. So one Wednesday afternoon, I drove the 50 miles to Bellevue and dropped in on my old nemesis.

Mr. Brown was extraordinarily polite. We chatted about the "business" I had come to discuss and then he walked me to my car. Before I drove off, he asked if he could call me. I said yes.

That was how our relationship started. In the coming weeks we had several dates, a number of long conversations, and more than a few stormy disagreements.

One date was especially memorable. We went out to dinner with a couple Paul had known since childhood. The man had retired from the military and had invited us to be his guests at the officers' club at Sandy Point naval base on Puget Sound. It was lovely and romantic. Music flowed from a jukebox in the corner, and Paul and I danced for hours. Finally, while Frank Sinatra sang "Strangers in the Night," Paul asked me to marry him.

I did what any love-struck 23-year-old would have done under the circumstances—I laughed.

I hadn't known him all that long, but I knew him well enough to know that he had a full complement of Irish mischief in his personality. The proposal, I was sure, was just part and parcel of the Paul Brown mystique—another bit of blarney. So I laughed.

But when Paul asked me again, and I could see in his eyes that he was sincere, I didn't laugh any more. I just looked back at him and said, "Yes."

Many people have been astounded by how brief our courtship was. I must admit that I sometimes look back on it in wonderment. But both Paul and I somehow knew from the start that we were like a hand in a glove, made for each other. I believe God had a hand in this from the beginning. In any case, over the next few weeks we had several serious conversations,

Above: Paul and I dating.

Right: My engagement photo.

which convinced me beyond a doubt that there was no one else in the entire world with whom I wanted to spend the rest of my life. I knew I now had two of the most wonderful men in the world deeply involved in my life.

I couldn't wait to tell my mother. She was my confidante, the only person I trusted with my deepest feelings, my fears, my dreams and the cares of my heart and soul. She was always a good listener and a wise counselor, a beacon of light in the darkness. Whenever I had something important to talk about, I always relied on her guidance and advice.

So when I called to tell her that Paul and I were engaged and planning to be married that December, I was eager to hear her response.

"Judie," she said at once, "this will never last. You haven't known him long enough."

As we talked, I understood her reservations more clearly. She had only met Paul once before, when I had brought him home for a weekend, and had been less than impressed. For

Our wedding day, December 30, 1967.

some reason Paul had been quiet around the family, almost withdrawn. Perhaps he was nervous, meeting the people he was planning to have as his in-laws. Perhaps he was just put off by the admittedly goofy sense of humor that prevailed in our home. In any case, he had not been himself, and my mother had come away convinced that he was not the man for me.

Even so, Mama respected my ability to make decisions for myself, and she was happy to see me so happy. In the end, she gave us her blessing.

The engagement was brief and occasionally stormy. My parents had the wedding announcements printed and in the mail when Paul and I had a huge argument one night and called the whole thing off. When I told Mama, she took it in stride. The cancellation notices, she assured me, could be in the mail within 72 hours. Fortunately it took Paul and me only 48 hours to make up, and the wedding was on again. Everything moved along peacefully from that point onward.

～

Barely three months after that magical evening at the naval base, Paul and I were married at the church in Hawthorne, California, where I had received my first Holy Communion as a little girl. The wedding had been planned long distance. My parents had moved back to California a few years before, and my mother's health had begun to deteriorate again, so I handled as many of the details as I could from Washington, where I was working.

I remember every detail of that day. The flowers were perfect, the church was magnificent, the priest was magnanimous, and magic filled the air. I remember wishing that my grandparents could have been there, as I knew they would have been pleased. I wished that my mother could have been completely healthy.

But most of all I remember my parents and the joy they exuded. Paul, who was proving to be one of the most complex and intriguing people I had ever known, had managed to endear himself to my family, and they couldn't have been happier for us. My parents had given so much and sacrificed so selflessly, not only for me but also for my sisters. Now they watched me begin a new family that I would always hope to model after the lessons I had learned in my own childhood. Their tears of joy were part of what made that day so perfect.

After a honeymoon in San Francisco, Paul and I set up housekeeping in a brand-new apartment in Seattle. A whole new phase of life was beginning for this obstinate woman of German descent and this marvelous man who reflected every character-istic for which the Irish are famous, from his grand sense of humor to his total dedication to family.

Chapter Five

New Baby, New Battle

~

1968–1970

The Lord keeps faith; he it is who will strengthen you and guard you against the evil one.

—*2 Thessalonians 3:3*

My first official action as Mrs. Paul A. Brown was to resign my position with K-Mart. The job still required a lot of travel, and Paul and I felt that wouldn't be good for our marriage. Paul himself had left the company a month before our wedding, because the prospect of relocating every six to eight months— not uncommon for those on the management track—seemed too disruptive. Besides, we had both grown attached to the Seattle area.

I took a job with the now-defunct White Front stores, a chain of discount retail outlets similar to K-Mart. I was head bookkeeper for their store in Tacoma. Paul entered management training with White Front, overseeing a store in Seattle. The two stores were 13 miles apart. We bought a small home about halfway between them, adopted a Weimaraner puppy, and began settling into married life.

But we did not settle into family life, precisely. We had decided to wait a while before having children. I went to a gynecologist to get a prescription for birth control pills. At this time, neither Paul nor I had any qualms about the pill; neither of us had been exposed to anything that would suggest that there was anything wrong, either medically or morally, with using it. For us, it was a simple proposition. We didn't want to start a family just yet, and taking the pill was the most effective way to prevent pregnancy.

There was only one problem.

After examining me, the gynecologist told me that it was a little late to be investigating birth control—I was already six weeks pregnant.

After the initial shock wore off, Paul and I were ecstatic. We picked out colors for the baby's room, began setting aside as much money as we could, and shared the good news with anyone who had a telephone. On November 23, 1968, after 12 hours of difficult labor, Hugh Richard Brown III was born. We named him after Paul's father, who had died before Paul and I met.

We did all the usual things that new parents do. We bought a crib and toys and a bassinet. We read every book we could get our hands on about what to do when the baby cried. We made faces about the dirty diapers and fumbled with the diaper pins. We did everything except have the baby baptized.

I had been a lukewarm Catholic, at best. Paul, though he had been raised a Catholic, had long since lost interest in the Church and for the first two years of our marriage refused to have anything to do with it.

I was a willing accomplice, to be sure, in our decision to ignore Sunday Mass. Paul and I would tell ourselves that Sunday was our only real time to be with the baby, so it made sense to skip church, stay home, and enjoy our little family. I occasionally put up token resistance, and I think Paul and I both knew our thinking was quite selfish. But in the end, when Sunday morning rolled around, we stayed home.

When Hugh was born, the subject of baptism came up briefly, but Paul vehemently refused even to consider it. He wouldn't have his child baptized into a faith he himself was not practicing. And that was that.

At the same time, because Hugh's birth had been a difficult one, the doctor recommended that I use the pill to avoid becoming pregnant again right away. My body was in a severely weakened state, he said, and another pregnancy following so soon after the first might have serious consequences. I needed time to recover, he said—at least two years.

By now I had read enough about the pill to have serious misgivings about its health consequences, so I asked if I could

Above: Our first wedding anniversary.

Right: Hugh Richard Brown III

use an IUD instead. My doctor, who was a practicing Catholic, approved my request and inserted the device without comment. He never told me that the IUD can cause abortion. He never suggested that I discuss the matter with a priest. In fact, he never said one word to me about the matter other than "okay."

This took place in January 1969. Hugh had been born two months before. *Humanae Vitae*, the Church's statement on birth control, had been issued eight months before. It is an indication of the state of my Catholicism that I had no idea the Church did not condone any artificial birth control, nor did anyone ever tell me this was the case. At that stage in my spiritual life, knowing the Church's position might not have mattered to me anyway. In any case, I got the IUD.

～

While Hugh was still an infant, Paul left White Front and became an insurance salesman. He worked with several different companies before settling in with one of the country's largest and best-known organizations. Almost immediately he became their top salesman.

One weekend Paul was in San Francisco, attending a sales seminar, when he called me late one night. He sounded excited. "Judie," he said, "I want you to make an appointment with the priest at the local parish. I want to go to confession and return to the Church."

I had no idea where this new line of thinking had come from. Perhaps Paul had been rethinking our conversations about baptizing Hugh, or the foolish ways we justified skipping Mass on Sundays. Perhaps someone at the seminar said something that challenged Paul to renew his faith—which, I believe, had never really died but had gone into "spiritual hibernation." I had no insight at all into the process. I only knew the result. We were going back to church.

Frankly, I was relieved. Despite all the reassurances we gave each other that what we were doing was okay, I knew in my heart that we had turned our backs on the Church—on the Lord—for no good reason other than laziness. I could never shake the nagging thought that if anything were to happen to either of us, we were headed straight for hell.

I had thought on more than one occasion of simply bundling up the baby and going to Mass by myself, but I was afraid Paul would be angry. During those early months and years of marriage, while we were still struggling to adjust to each other, I guess I was insecure enough that I didn't want to provoke any disagreements that might turn into fights that might turn into separation and divorce. Silly, perhaps, but that was what I feared might happen. That, plus a heavy dose of my own lukewarm attitude, was more than enough to keep me away from church.

But Paul's phone call changed everything. I contacted the pastor, Father Willonberg, the very next morning. I explained to him that both Paul and I wanted to come back to church, wanted to make a general confession and receive the sacraments, and wanted to have our son baptized. He didn't bat an eye, God bless him.

Soon all the arrangements were made. We visited Father Willonberg and made our confessions. What a feeling of warmth and security. The next Sunday we went to Mass. Hugh, now 18 months old, was baptized that morning. Not too many babies are able to walk forward to be baptized, wearing a suit, and chatting with the priest all the while, but that's how it was for Hugh. We had called the couple who had hosted us for that fateful dinner at the naval officers' club and asked them to be Hugh's godparents. All in all, it was quite a week.

It was also at this time that I had the IUD removed—not because of any convictions about either its abortifacient properties or the Church's position on birth control; we were still ignorant on those topics. We had simply decided that we wanted to have more children and didn't want to wait. I had recovered sufficiently from Hugh's birth that the health risk was largely removed, and I had taken quite well to being a full-time wife and mother. Paul and I decided we wanted six children, and we couldn't wait to get started. By the next summer, Baby Brown number two was on the way.

By this time we were attending Mass regularly. In fact, it was while we were at Mass one Sunday that Father Willonberg said something that would turn our lives upside down.

He spoke, with great distress, of a referendum question that was to be on the ballot in the state of Washington that November—a referendum to liberalize the state's abortion law.

Abortion. In those days the word still had the power to shock people, and it shocked Paul and me that Sunday morning. Here we were, brand-new parents with another baby on the way, newly returned to the faith of our childhood, hearing a sermon about people who wanted to kill little babies with the full consent of the law. It felt as though the earth had moved under our pew. How, I wondered, could a mother willfully seek the destruction of her own child?

I was soon to find out, however, that there were many women who thought nothing of it, who thought that their own sexual freedom should supersede any other claims, who thought they should have the right to do away with the "problems" created by their own choices and actions.

So when Father Willonberg invited us to work with him, distributing pro-life literature door to door and asking our neighbors and friends to be sure to vote "no" on Referendum 20, Paul and I were eager to get involved. That was the beginning of our battle to save little children like our own.

~

Today, years later, people often tell me how inane the arguments of the pro-death forces seem to them. In 1970, in the state of Washington, the arguments were exactly the same. Then, as now, there were people who believed that not all human beings were created equal and that the law should permit some human beings to murder other human beings when it suited their convenience. People were just as selfish and depraved then as they are now.

The only difference is that then there were no organized pro-life groups ready and willing to fight for the rights of the pre-born. Just five months after our ragtag group began its door-to-door campaign, the people of Washington said "yes" to abortion.

We were crushed. How could it have happened? Where would it end? How could we stop it?

Chapter Six

Blessed Are the Poor

1970–1972

I was hard pressed and was falling, but the Lord helped me. My strength and my courage is the Lord, and he has been my savior.

—Psalm 118:13–14

As it turned out, the 1970 referendum defeat in Washington was far from the only blow our family was to suffer that year. They say that adversity is a great teacher. Well, the Lord chose 1970 to shower us with painful lessons.

That summer, amid the frenetic door-to-door literature campaign, we took a Sunday afternoon off and went to a company picnic. A lot of the dads were taking their kids down an especially high, steep slide on the playground. Paul took Hugh down the slide a couple of times, much to their mutual delight. For some reason, on the third time down they picked up more speed than before. Afraid that he might drop Hugh onto the concrete playground surface, Paul clutched him tightly with both arms and then tried to stop by digging his heels into the hard surface.

The result was a shattered kneecap, several weeks in and out of the hospital, a full leg cast for six months, and an inability to pursue his career as a salesman. On top of that came the sudden realization that, although he was the number-one salesman for a major insurance company, Paul had never sold himself a disability policy.

Because he worked strictly on commission, this meant no income for our family. Here we were with one baby and another on the way, a mortgage, two car payments, a pile of credit card

Above: Hugh teasing Cathy.

Left: Me, Paul, Cathy at five months and two-and-a-half-year-old Hugh.

bills, and no way to pay them. What followed was humbling and anguishing—but in God's master plan, much to our benefit.

I had some unemployment insurance coming to me, for which I applied. Paul received a small check as well. We quickly learned how to survive on $20 a week for groceries. When we fell hopelessly behind with our bills, we filed for bankruptcy and homesteaded our house, a legal maneuver that enabled us to stay in our home without bank foreclosure until we could regain a steady income and pay down our debts.

In time, we did exactly that. But the intervening six months were just awful. I am still grateful to our neighbors, who really pitched in and helped us. They understood our predicament and were there for us. Not once did they speak or act in a way that added to the embarrassment I knew Paul was feeling. And to think it all happened because he took his son down a playground slide one summer afternoon.

Paul started to go stir crazy more than once during that period. The combination of boredom and frustration was almost more than he could handle. But he never lost his perspective. I was the one who did that. I would burst into tears over what I saw as the hopelessness of our situation. Having worked as a credit manager for so many different stores, the idea of declaring personal bankruptcy was especially galling to me. But Paul would firmly assure me that we would survive and that we would never experience such an ordeal again, as long as he had anything to say about it.

∼

Paul was still in the midst of his rehabilitation when the second little Brown made her appearance on the scene. We were having Sunday brunch at a neighbor's house—a short stack of pancakes with peach preserves—when the first labor pangs hit. Remembering how long the labor process had been with Hugh, I wasn't overly concerned. I casually mentioned to Paul that after breakfast we should probably consider starting off for the hospital.

We very nearly didn't make it. Catherine Marie Brown (named for her two grandmothers) was born just three hours later. Paul was present for the delivery and was the first one to hold her—the nurses cleaned her up and presented her to him with a tiny pink bow in her hair. He was one proud father. "Judie, I was really praying for a girl," he told me. "I'm the youngest of four boys, so I especially wanted a daughter."

Cathy's big brother was also quite enthusiastic upon her arrival home. He could hardly wait to hold her, feed her, give her a bath and do anything else I was willing to let him try. Actually, life was quite a panic in the Brown household during those first few weeks. Between the new baby, little Hugh—who was only two and a half—and Paul, who was still hobbled by his knee injury, it was hard to keep track of just exactly who was taking care of whom. We even had neighbors dropping in to help Hugh help Paul take care of Cathy so that I could take care of everything else. If you think it sounds confusing, you should have been there to see it.

Two months after Cathy was born I went back to the doctor, and to our pastor, to discuss birth control. The danger still existed with regard to my health. My womb had been seriously weakened during Cathy's delivery, and my body was too weak to withstand another pregnancy any time soon. So, with the blessing of a Catholic priest and a doctor who was also a Catholic, I once again used an IUD.

It astonishes me now, looking back on the experience, that both our priest and our doctor were either ignorant of what the Catholic Church teaches on birth control, or simply delinquent in their duty to tell young couples the truth. For my part, I had no idea I was doing anything that the Church taught was wrong. How was I to know, if the only people who could have told me, didn't? No one ever told me that IUDs were supposed to be painless, so when this one caused me discomfort I didn't think anything of it. Maybe it was the Lord's way of trying to penetrate my ignorance, to let me know something was amiss. If so, I missed the hint.

∼

The day finally came when Paul was able to walk again without assistance. He told me he wanted to return to K-Mart and resume his career there, if he could, though it would likely mean moving away from our home and our friends. I wasn't eager to pull up stakes and start over in a strange place, but we talked it over thoroughly and I finally told Paul that if going back to K-Mart was what he thought was right, then I was with him.

K-Mart welcomed him back and promptly offered him an attractive management position—in Atlanta, Georgia. What a shock. Here we were with two little children, a terrific job offer, and no money for a cross-country move.

We borrowed from every relative who had a dollar to spare, bought a used 1957 Dodge that gave new meaning to the word "clunker," piled our two little babies and our large German shepherd into the back, and hit the road. We decided to go by way of Los Angeles, so that my parents could see the babies and so that my master-mechanic stepfather could fix up the car that was going to have to carry us to what seemed like the other side of the earth.

Our two weeks in Los Angeles were marvelous. My parents were delighted to spend so much time with their grandchildren, even though my mother's arthritis had advanced and she had great difficulty holding a baby for any length of time. I had the sinking feeling that she would soon be completely unable to move. But we did all we could to make our visit special for her.

From Los Angeles we set off on our trek. We crossed the southern tier of the country, finally arriving in Savannah, Georgia, on the Atlantic coast. Paul's mother and oldest brother lived there, and the kids and I bunked with them while Paul went on to Atlanta to find a place for us to live. Three weeks later we moved into a small, dirty, run-down rental house, got our furniture and belongings out of storage, and settled in to our new life. It wasn't much, but it was home.

~

Because we needed additional income, I took care of other people's children during the day—and sometimes for a couple of weeks at a time when their parents had to travel out of town on business. I was also able to volunteer on behalf of the local chapter of Birthright, which worked to provide housing for women who were pregnant and who might otherwise seek an abortion. I was able to collect items for Birthright baby showers while keeping the children in the car.

I soon came in contact with the leaders of Georgia Right to Life, a fledgling group just gearing up in early 1973. I assembled newsletters, stuffed them into envelopes, and dropped them off at the post office.

Gradually things began to turn around for the Brown family. Paul's salary from K-Mart pulled us out of debt once and for all. It also enabled me to stop baby-sitting—a real blessing, as our own children needed more of my time.

I also increased my involvement with Birthright and with Georgia Right to Life. The Supreme Court had recently issued its infamous *Roe v. Wade* and *Doe v. Bolton* decisions, which threw out the abortion laws of all 50 states and guaranteed abortion on demand. Working for the pro-life cause now seemed to Paul and me to be a moral imperative.

Though Paul was working 70 to 80 hours a week, he always made time to keep abreast of what was happening in the movement. There was a lot of optimism in those days that Congress would swiftly overturn the Supreme Court's reckless action. Paul thought that optimism was naive and foresaw a national tragedy of enormous proportions if abortion were indeed allowed to remain legal. I'm sad to say he turned out to be absolutely correct.

◇

Before long Paul was promoted to a senior management position. As always, a promotion meant relocation. This time we were off to Kannapolis, North Carolina, where, among other things, we finally learned what the Catholic Church really taught about birth control.

I know it is difficult to understand how we remained ignorant of this teaching for so long. The truth, I suppose, is that we didn't really want to know. We had been raised Catholic, and we understood the basics of the creed and the sacraments. We were going to Mass every Sunday and raising our children as good Catholics. In the early years of our marriage, when we sought out our pastor and a Catholic physician for advice on the subject of birth control, they simply told us what they thought we wanted to hear—that taking the pill, or using an IUD, was acceptable—second best, perhaps, but still okay.

Our lack of understanding isn't all that surprising. I still run into many people who, despite being lifelong Catholics, don't understand anything more about the Church's teaching in this area than we did.

But when our pastor in Kannapolis finally shared with us the Church's full teaching about the sanctity of marriage, the full meaning of the procreative act, and the evil of birth control as a denial of trust in God, we didn't hesitate. I stopped using the IUD, once and for all.

Our move to Kannapolis signaled the start of new era in our lives. It signaled many other changes as well.

Chapter Seven

In the School
of Adversity

~

1973–1974

Dismiss all anxiety from your minds.
Present your needs to God in every form
of prayer and in petitions full of gratitude.
Then God's own peace, which is beyond
all understanding, will stand guard over
your hearts and minds, in Christ Jesus.
—Philippians 4:6–7

Talk about sending a lamb into the lion's den! We had barely unpacked the moving crates when I suddenly found myself
engaged in a public debate with Kannapolis' leading proponent
of abortion.

It started innocently enough. We had been getting
acquainted with our parish priest, who was trying to raise the
parish's awareness of abortion. He thought a public debate
with the local abortionist would be a good idea. When he
heard of my past involvement with Birthright and Georgia
Right to Life, he decided I would be the perfect person to represent the pro-life side. And for some reason I'll never understand, I agreed to do it.

Remember, I had no training in debate, and no experience
at it either. And by this time our third little one was on the way.
All I'd ever done as a pro-life volunteer was to stuff envelopes
and transport items to garage sales. My opponent, whom I will
call "Dr. Crosby" (it's not his real name), was one of the most
highly respected obstetrician/gynecologists in the area. He
obviously wasn't too intimidated at the prospect of debating a
pregnant housewife from the rental district of Kannapolis.
What would someone like me know about the complex issues
surrounding abortion?

I knew hardly anything about the complex issues, so I stuck
to the simple ones. When my turn came to speak, I simply
described what actually happens to a baby during an abortion.
This so unnerved Dr. Crosby that he got up and walked out of
the room.

Lesson number one in Kannapolis: God uses those who are
willing to be used, and He gives them whatever they need to
accomplish the task He sets before them.

∼

Life continued to be chaotic, even beyond the usual disrup-
tions caused by moving. I had to go to work again to send Hugh,
who was now five, to a Christian kindergarten. I eventually
found a job managing heating oil accounts for a local company.
It only required a few hours a day, which left me plenty of time
to be home with Cathy.

But then we got an unexpected call. My mother was gravely ill. Somehow Paul scraped up enough money for me to fly home to California to see her. She was in the hospital with severe arthritis and bleeding ulcers, and at first I really thought it would be our last visit.

Mama eventually pulled through, but it required eight months in the hospital. By the time she came home, she had lost her ability to walk. This was a real blow to someone who had always done everything for everybody else. For a time she was extremely bitter. But Daddy was always there for her, loving her as much as ever, always patient, always kind.

I have always looked back on my stepfather's conduct during this time as a prime example of Christlike love, being willing to take up the cross, with all its pain, for the sake of the joy that lies on the other side of self-sacrifice. My stepfather never formally professed any religion. But I think he lived the Gospel message better than many of us, who claim to know the way to salvation.

That was lesson number two during this trying period—God loves a cheerful giver, and He blesses those who face hardship with faith, patience and dignity.

~

Finally, life appeared to be settling down. I was back from California and, as my pregnancy entered the seventh month, I left my job with the heating oil company to prepare for the arrival of Baby Brown number three.

At the first sign of labor, we rushed to the hospital on June 17th for what we were sure would be a speedy labor and delivery.

But the 18th came, the labor escalated and then dropped off, and no baby. The 19th came. Again the labor escalated. Again it dropped. Still, no baby. All this time I was in a labor room with a bunch of wires taped to my tummy, monitoring the baby's heartbeat. After three days of false starts, the heartbeat had begun to grow quite weak. The doctors—and Paul and I, as well—were starting to get worried.

It soon became clear that the baby was in distress and this required immediate action. Fortunately, Paul and I were told, the most accomplished doctor in the area happened to be on duty that night. He would be the best person to handle the situation. We couldn't be in better hands—my old debate foe, Dr. Crosby.

At that point, I really wasn't thinking about the debate, and Dr. Crosby was far too professional to let our past encounter color his attitudes. He sized up the situation and ordered an immediate Caesarian section. I wasn't too excited about the prospect of major surgery, but after three days of labor I just wanted that baby to be born.

What I didn't realize then was just how serious the situation really was. Paul and Dr. Crosby had been discussing the possibility that the baby would be stillborn. Given my history of difficult childbirth, and the prolonged labor I had already endured this time around, Dr. Crosby was concerned that I might not survive, either. I can only imagine the agony that Paul must have suffered, pacing outside that operating room, awaiting the outcome of the operation.

As it turned out, he needn't have worried. The most skilled surgeon in the state delivered Christina Lee Brown at 9:37 p.m. on June 19. We had intended to name her Nancy, but in view of all that had happened, we thought Christina was a better reflection of our gratitude to the Lord. We named her Lee in honor of the woman who had suggested, several years before, that I meet Paul Brown.

Christy was beautiful and perfectly healthy. The only ill effect I suffered was an infection, which prevented me from holding her for five days. That was difficult. But once I learned how grave the situation had been, waiting a few days to hold my baby didn't seem like such a hardship after all.

I had a fairly long recovery from Christy's birth. I spent part of my time writing to each of the hospital staff who had been so helpful to us during our long ordeal. I even wrote a letter to the editor of the local newspaper, praising Dr. Crosby's expertise. When I went in for my six-week checkup, I took Christy with me and asked Dr. Crosby if he would like to come out and see her. He looked at me in a very strange way and said simply, "No. I can't."

I puzzled over his response for a long time. In retrospect, I suppose he must have been struggling with the conflict between his obvious talent for saving life and his conviction that it was all right to take life at the whim of the mother. Did it occur to him—as it certainly did to me—that had I been on another floor of the hospital that night, he would have been killing Christy rather than saving her?

I don't know. I never had another opportunity to talk to him. I do know that at last report Dr. Crosby was no longer doing abortions but was devoting much of his time to specializing in women with distressed pregnancies. I still pray for him and for all abortionists, that their hearts may be softened.

Lesson number three: God can use times of trial to touch the hardest of hearts. Thus it was, I believe, that He used Christy and me to encourage Dr. Crosby to move a few steps forward in his awareness of the sanctity of life.

~

When Christy was eight months old, Paul was transferred to Steubenville, Ohio—his first job as manager of his own store. This transfer took effect immediately, which meant that the family was left behind. Paul flew to Steubenville one Monday morning to get acquainted with his staff, take over operations at the store, and start looking for a home for us.

The very next day Christy developed a fever—a very high fever. Her temperature went up to 105 degrees. I called the pediatrician, who suggested I give her an alcohol bath. Her tempera-

Hugh at five years,
Cathy at three years and
Christy at four months.

ture went down for a while, but spiked again a few hours later. I
gave her another alcohol bath, and her temperature went down
as it had before. Unfortunately, it also went back up again. By
three in the morning she was in convulsions, and I was in a
panic. I frantically called neighbors until I was able to borrow a
car and find someone to watch the other kids. Then I raced off to
the hospital, praying all the while that Christy would be all right.

When we arrived, the emergency room staff took Christy
from me, rushed her into an examining room with the doors
slamming shut behind them, and didn't communicate with me
again for several hours. When the doctor finally came out, his
expression was grim. Christy was now in a coma. They had
given her a spinal tap, fearing that she might have spinal meningitis. If that were the case, she might not survive.

For two days, little Christy, with an IV in her head, lay in her
crib in the intensive care unit without moving. I was beside
myself. The worst part was that I had been unable to communicate with Paul. Since we were in the process of moving, our
home phone had been disconnected. I had to rely on the assistant manager of the local K-Mart store to convey messages to
Paul at the Steubenville store. Though I sent several urgent messages, for some reason no one even tried to contact him until the
third day, when Christy finally came out of the coma.

It happened just that suddenly, too. Three days after I had
rushed her to the hospital, she woke up, her temperature
returned to normal, and she broke out in a bright red rash from
head to toe. Her problem was not spinal meningitis, but a case
of roseola.

Lesson number four: In our weakest moments, in the midst
of our most terrible fears, when we feel most alone—even then
our Lord is at our side, working His will in our lives. Without
Paul there to lead me, I had to handle Christy's crisis all alone. I
learned, for the first time, that I did indeed have the strength to
cope with such an ordeal.

∼

By the time Paul finally got word of Christy's condition, she
was already out of danger. By the time he got back to Kannapolis
to be with us, I was more than ready to leave.

There were so many tests in such a short period of time that I occasionally doubted my ability to cope. I can remember crying, then laughing, then crying again, wanting nothing more than to hang onto my husband and never let him out of my sight. Even though we had survived it all, I never wanted to go through it again. I just wanted to tell Paul how much I loved him and how much I hoped we would never be separated again.

Chapter Eight

Hello, Congressman

≈

1975–1976

*I give you my word, if you are ready to
believe that you will receive whatever you
ask for in prayer, it shall be done for you.*
                                    —Mark 11:24

We had been attending our new parish in Steubenville for about three months when a notice appeared in the bulletin announcing a pro-life meeting. Upper Ohio Valley Right to Life was looking for new members. This was 1975, and even though the *Roe v. Wade* decision had been in force for more than two years, awareness of the reality of child killing still had not sifted down to the grassroots level of American life, even among Christians.

At the meeting, the leaders mentioned that they needed an editor for the newsletter. I volunteered. They also needed to find a local business that would let them sell pro-life Christmas cards on the sidewalk. Paul offered the K-Mart store that he managed. The card sale was a great success, and opened the way to bake sales, a flea market, and many other activities that raised funds for our group and helped us spread the word about the plight of the preborn.

I was soon chosen to represent our chapter at meetings of the Ohio Right to Life Society, which is where I met the man who really taught me how to be an articulate pro-life spokesman— our state chairman, Dr. John C. Willke. He spoke with eloquence and ease. He emphasized the sanctity of all life and the child's right to life from the moment of conception, and he emphasized the importance of faith in doing pro-life work.

~

In January 1976, Upper Ohio Valley Right to Life asked me to go to the March for Life in Washington and to represent them at a special breakfast with members of Congress.

The trip to Washington was definitely a special occasion. The day before the march, I went to a meeting sponsored by the March for Life Corporation. The president, Nellie Gray, spoke brilliantly about standing for our principles, about God's blessing of new life and about our call to be soldiers in the war against innocent preborn children. That speech made such an impact on me that, whenever I think of it, the same feelings of excitement and resolve well up within me. I wanted to do more for the preborn. I wanted to be closer to the action. That night I prayed that our Lord would somehow make it happen. It was a fateful prayer.

The next day I had breakfast with our congressman, Wayne Hayes. He was getting a lot of unfavorable publicity at the time, because of his cavorting with his attractive "secretary," Elizabeth Ray. Though I was less than impressed with his commitment to family values, I had learned from my experience with Dr. Crosby that God never gives up on anyone. So I talked my head off that morning about the babies and the need to protect them. He listened politely, and then gave his political justification for doing nothing. It was a speech I was to hear many times, in many forms, from many politicians over the years.

Frustrated by my encounter with Congressman Hayes, but still invigorated by the March for Life and especially by Nellie Gray, I arrived back in Steubenville on fire for the pro-life cause. I told Paul I had prayed that he would be transferred to the Washington area. His response was immediate and emphatic: "That is the last —— place on earth I'd ever want to live."

Two weeks later Paul was transferred. Care to guess where?

Paul fussed and stewed about it, but eventually he accepted the transfer. It was a promotion, which meant more prestige within the company, more money, and better benefits. I called Dr. Willke and told him of our impending move. He promised to introduce me to Dr. Mildred Jefferson, the president of the National Right to Life Committee.

~

It had been an eventful year in Steubenville—a year that launched Paul and me into pro-life work once and for all. We had learned a lot. Now we stood on the brink of what we sensed would be a grand adventure.

Chapter Nine

Mrs. Brown Goes to Washington

∾

1976–1979

Where there is jealousy and strife, there also are inconstancy and all kinds of vile behavior. Wisdom from above, by contrast, is first of all innocent. It is also peaceable, lenient, docile, rich in sympathy and the kindly deeds that are its fruits, impartial and sincere. The harvest of justice is sown in peace for those who cultivate peace.

—James 3:16–18

We moved to Washington with the usual Brown family flair—Cathy, Christy, Hugh and I all had the chicken pox. If you are an adult who has never had the chicken pox, I don't recommend it. I was quite sick. Poor Paul had to take care of everyone, right in the midst of getting settled in a new home and a new job.

In time, life got back to normal (whatever "normal" is for a crew like ours). Paul had found a townhouse for us in Woodbridge, Virginia, about 30 miles south of Washington. Hugh and Cathy started school—Cathy was in kindergarten now—and Christy stayed home with me.

But I didn't stay home for long. In April 1976 I ventured into the city to visit the offices of National Right to Life and to meet with Dr. Mildred Jefferson and the rest of the staff. "The rest of the staff" turned out to be only two other people. It seemed that the executive director had left several months before and had not yet been replaced. Activity was at an all-time low. Even the remaining two women had little to do because the phones seldom rang and practically no mail came in.

Dr. Jefferson still had a dynamic vision of NRLC as an umbrella organization under which all the other pro-life efforts in the country could come together. And she still had a tremendous flair with the media. What she needed was someone with business experience, someone who could shape things up, get things moving and put a spark into the operation—someone like me. Before I knew it I had signed on.

On one hand, it was a dream come true. I would be able to do the thing that meant more to me than anything else in the world—help save the babies. And I would be able to do it alongside Dr. Jefferson.

On the other hand, I still had three small children, ages 8, 6 and 3. Until now I had considered myself a full-time, stay-at-home mom. Working full time outside the house was not what I had bargained for. But the opportunity proved too tempting to resist. I put all three kids in a private school.

It was, to say the least, stressful. I was able to carpool into the city with Paul and two others, but it meant leaving the house at 6 A.M. We got back home at 6 P.M., after stopping to pick up the kids.

I maintained this pace for two years. During that time, we significantly enhanced the effectiveness of NRLC. We grew to 20 employees and six times the office space, and gained greater national prominence. I was consumed with it. I worked at home on nights and weekends, giving up every waking hour that wasn't directly taken up with immediate family necessities. Looking back, I have to say it wasn't worth the price I paid by putting my vocation to the pro-life cause—important as it was—ahead of my vocation as a wife and mother.

Finally I had to scale back. We bought a new house 10 miles farther away from the city. The logistics of travel and childcare, which had always been ridiculously complicated, now became simply impossible. And besides, it was time to make my own life correspond to my pro-family convictions by becoming a real wife and mother again.

I told Dr. Jefferson I was putting my kids (now 10, 8 and 5) in a normal parish school and that I would be leaving the office at two o'clock every afternoon so I could be there when they got home. I was going to clean the house and do the laundry and cook dinner again. She consented without hesitation. I felt a great sense of relief.

It didn't last long. Things were changing for Paul, just as they had for me.

~

Paul had outgrown the opportunities available to him with K-Mart, and he wanted to get away from the pressure, the 80-hour weeks, and the constant specter of having to pull up stakes and relocate every year or two. Like me, he longed for a more normal home life. And, like me, he wanted to do more for the babies.

A few months before, Paul had helped start something called the Life Amendment Political Action Committee, or LAPAC. Its goal was to mobilize money, manpower and political clout against pro-abortion political candidates, and to support candidates who were pro-life.

The idea had come from the noble, but doomed, presidential campaign of Ellen McCormack in 1976. Paul, who was a great student of politics and a fanatic about the need for effective political action on behalf of the pro-life cause, greatly admired Mrs. McCormack and her band of dedicated supporters. They had shown how far a determined candidate could go, carrying the message of the sanctity of life on a shoestring budget. Surely, Paul thought, a national political action committee could do the same kind of thing across the country, by doing nothing more than publicizing the various candidates' stand on abortion.

Paul and the other LAPAC founders—Robert L. Sassone, Sr., and Morton Downey, Jr. (yes, the infamous television talk-show host)—were passionately committed to making a difference for the babies, but all had full-time jobs. They and their small group of volunteers were extremely limited in what they could accomplish.

But all that changed one Sunday evening when Paul went to Mass. The kids were sick and we were going to Mass on "split shifts," so Paul was by himself. When he came home, he simply announced that he was resigning his job the next morning. Without a moment's hesitation I replied, "Great!"

He later told me it was the sermon that had moved him to take such a bold step. The theme had been, "The only things of value in this life are the things you can take with you into eternity." He realized, he said, that he didn't want to retire from a company where his main achievement was keeping his toothpaste displays in order. Being a store manager, despite its prestige and good pay, was not fulfilling his desire to make his mark on the

People *magazine featured Paul and me and the work of LAPAC in its January 22, 1979 issue.*

world, so that his children might have a better and more loving place to raise their families. And besides, he pointed out, America was killing one and a half-million babies a year. It had to stop.

Paul took a gamble and decided to put all his time and energy into developing LAPAC. Fundraising was the first priority. As he often said, in addition to backing pro-life candidates and giving the pro-life movement the political credibility it so desperately needed, he had a family to feed. It was clear from the start that Paul had a knack for raising the needed money. His strategy for LAPAC resounded with grassroots America. It also pleased the board of NRLC. NRLC had no political action committee of its own at the time and was glad to see one forming. Paul invited Felicia Goeken and Ellen Dempsey from the NRLC board to serve on the LAPAC Board. Mrs. Goeken was instrumental in starting the first pro-life voter ID programs. NRLC's board of directors trusted Paul and his compatriots—at least at first. In addition, LAPAC gained expert advice from political strategists, and LAPAC quickly got on the move.

LAPAC almost immediately discovered the astute, wise and fearless leadership qualities in heroic pro-lifers like Ellen Dempsey of South Dakota, Mary Ellen McCaffrey of California and Norm and Mary Weslin of Colorado. This is the same man who came to be known later as Father Norm Weslin, founder of the Lambs of Christ. Mary, Norm's late wife, is remembered with loving affection by many of us. These people wanted to make a difference in politics and were willing to contribute time and

NRLC Convention Chicago, June 18, 1977.

energy in outrageous proportion just for the sake of doing God's work in politics. These were the people who inspired Paul, Sean and Bob to get LAPAC moving.

Its impact was felt as early as the 1978 election campaign. One of LAPAC's target races was in Iowa, where Senator Dick Clark was running for re-election. Earlier in the year, a young man named Paul Litke had walked across the country, carrying a very large and heavy cross, and asking everyone he met to join with him in praying and acting against the crime of abortion. Paul Brown remembered Litke's fervor and asked if he would take up the cross again, and walk across Iowa, following pro-abortion Senator Clark everywhere he went. Clark always walked his state in search of votes, but never before had he done so with a shadow like Paul Litke. The strategy worked, and Clark lost his race.

LAPAC helped defeat several additional pro-abortion senators, such as Birch Bayh of Indiana and George McGovern of South Dakota. My husband appeared on numerous national television programs, and NBC even ran a segment about LAPAC during "Weekend," its popular news and features program. People magazine ran a four-page feature on me, Paul and our three children. All in all, it was a dramatic step forward for the pro-life movement. Finally we would be taken seriously in the political arena for our ability to help elect—and more importantly defeat—candidates for office.

~

My world began to collapse just as Paul's was coming together. Trouble was brewing at NRLC. Some of the leadership wanted to co-opt LAPAC, bringing it under NRLC control. Paul would have none of it; he and the other board members felt that independence was a key to LAPAC's effectiveness. That led to some strained relationships at NRLC.

At the same time, I became more aware of various internal struggles at NRLC. When Dr. Jefferson left in June 1978, I realized the degree to which she had been protecting me from NRLC's internal politics. She did such a masterful job of protecting me that she failed to see the coup coming that ultimately resulted in her being tossed out without apology.

NRLC suffered from the usual sort of infighting and power struggles that occur in any organization—fifty zealous, energetic human beings served on the board of directors. But it discouraged me just the same. Paul urged me to stay on and try to make a difference. But by early 1979, it was clear to me that I simply had to leave.

The new regime found fault with my early departure to pick up my children from school. I was told, "Make other arrangements. What you are doing is not professional."

When one of the officers entered the office one day to find my little one, Christy, with me at work, you would have thought that child was an alien. I was told never to bring a child to the office again. Wow, and that from a pro-life leader? I was amazed.

And there was the matter of the *People* magazine article and the NBC program. As one NRLC officer said to me, "Why did you permit that crew to film your family praying?" Another officer challenged me for agreeing to do the program. She said I never should have given a public interview, but should have deferred to her instead. I was instructed never, ever to give an interview again.

As if all this wasn't bad enough, I found myself increasingly unable to support NRLC's views on a number of key issues. As far as I was concerned, there was no such thing as compromise when trying to save babies. That was the lesson I had learned from people I admired and had grown to trust. For example, Nellie Gray's words the night before my first March for Life experience in 1976 rang in my ears: "We may not compromise with the life of even one baby. There are no exceptions; there is no compromise where human life is concerned."

Dr. Mildred Jefferson often told me that God never abandons those who are faithful to His little ones. And while it is clear that she could have received immense financial rewards had she chosen to make personal prestige and comfort her life's goals, the fact that her commitment to pro-life principle always came first impressed me more than words can say.

Likewise, Father Paul Marx constantly challenged anyone who even remotely suggested that politics had to be taken into account before one decided whether or not to stand up and proclaim the full truth regarding the sanctity of human life. He was intolerant of those who repeatedly argued that contraception and abortion were not related and should not be opposed with equal fervor by the pro-life movement. He spoke passionately on the undeniable relationship between the two. I can remember his admonition that those who chose to avoid the obvious were doomed to defeat. He never shrank from this view, even when others attacked him for being *unrealistic* and *divisive*.

When I sought advice from Dr. Murray Norris, one of my dearest friends, he was unflinching. As the publisher of the first ever pro-life newspaper and countless books and tracts exposing the evils of the day, he knew precisely what to say to me. He warned me that the religion of secular humanism had crept into the philosophy of those who put pragmatism before the laws of God. He said that if I remained, I too would fall prey to the wicked allure of doing "what is possible" rather than "what is right." And he said something I shall never forget—"Judie, never serve man without first discerning what God wants."

These dear friends and allies in the pro-life struggle inspired me and helped me formulate a philosophy that does not allow for equivocation when a human being's life is on the line. God had given me role models, and so it would not be difficult to resign from NRLC. In fact, it was painfully clear that I could no longer claim to adhere to moral absolutes while working for an organization that did not. The National Right to Life Committee was disconcertingly silent on such subjects as abortifacient birth control and the contraceptive mentality. The political strategy they were pursuing then, and even now, leaves the door open for some surgical abortion. When rape, incest and threat to the life of the mother are tolerated as excuses for rationalizing abortion, there is no way any organization is going to bite the bullet and oppose contraception.

My discernment process included lengthy conversations with Father Denis O'Brien, M.M., a priest it had been my good fortune to meet during a National Right to Life Committee convention in Boston in 1976. As I look back on that first meeting, I am amazed at the brazen attitude I displayed.

Father O'Brien entered the media room at the convention, and walked up to me, since I was the person in charge. He asked me a question, but I didn't answer him. I looked at him and said, "Father, I am sorry, but this is the press room, and you are not a member of the press, so would you please leave?"

He politely smiled, and said, "Young lady, you should know better than to speak to a priest in that tone. Now, would you please answer my question?"

Father O'Brien became the strongest influence in my life when it came to morality, ethics or prudence. Father O'Brien became my most trusted advisor, and eventually agreed to serve as American Life League's spiritual director. It was Father O'Brien who confirmed what others had advised me to do and said, "Judie, it's about time you left." In March 1979, I resigned from the National Right to Life Committee.

I want to make clear that I have never judged any individual at NRLC as being anything less than totally committed to the proposition that every abortion is murder and must be stopped. But I was unhappy with NRLC's strategy in pursuing its corporate aims. I was afraid their approach would make it too easy for politicians to get away with statements such as "I am personally opposed to abortion, but..." and "I am against abortion, except..." To my way of thinking, there can be no "buts" and no "excepts" when it comes to saving the babies. If we retreat from the absolute truth, if we start settling for the acceptance of some killing, then our effectiveness is ended and our movement is dead.

Strangely enough, my letter of resignation, carefully written and sent to every National Right to Life Committee board member, did not generate any formal response. There was dead silence, so dead that I discussed the matter with an attorney. Based on past observations of the way in which some NRLC leaders treated fellow pro-lifers, I had reason to be concerned. I wanted to make absolutely certain that my resignation letter would not be used to discredit my reputation as a pro-lifer. Experience had taught me that when dealing with NRLC, an ounce of prevention is definitely worth a pound of cure.

Chapter Ten

A Telegram from Heaven

~

1979–1980

*Trust in the Lord with all your heart, on
your own intelligence rely not; In all your
ways be mindful of him, and he will make
straight your paths.*

—Proverbs 3:5–6

It was on March 1, 1979, that I dropped my letter of resignation in the mail to NRLC. The sound of that letter hitting the bottom of the mailbox seemed to trigger the most extraordinary sequence of events I had ever experienced. It was as if the Lord had been waiting to communicate with me about what He wanted me to do next, and my leaving NRLC made that communication possible. I have always referred to the entire experience as "receiving a telegram from heaven."

Paul and I had been invited to a reception in Washington the afternoon I mailed my resignation letter. I recall phoning Paul to tell him what I had just done and that I was on my way to meet him. While I was driving downtown, Paul got another phone call. It was from Morton Blackwell, who at the time was an associate of the conservative direct-mail fundraising guru, Richard Viguerie. He said that Mr. Viguerie was interested in providing start-up funds for a new pro-life group and was looking for someone to head the effort. I was Mr. Viguerie's first choice, Morton said, but they knew I was loyally committed to NRLC, and wondered if we might be able to recommend someone else.

Paul just laughed. "Morton," he said, "you're not going to believe this!"

∽

That is how the odyssey of American Life Lobby and American Life League began.

Within a month I had met with Mr. Viguerie to discuss ideas. We engaged an attorney to help with the paperwork, and met several times with our pro-life friends, Robert L. Sassone, Sr., and Gabrielle Avery. Sitting around the dining room table in our home, we selected a name for our new organization. We invited Gabrielle's husband, Walter, to serve as its first treasurer. We also directed our lawyer to start drawing up the incorporation papers.

The story of our lawyer and how we found him is another tale of God's infinite mercy and love for His babies. During my years at NRLC I had grown to know and admire Paul Weyrich, founder of the Free Congress Foundation. He was the host of several important meetings in Washington, and I represented NRLC at some of them. When I left NRLC and decided that ALL was going to become a reality, Paul and I also decided that having an attorney was a must. So one morning we discussed this need with Mr. Weyrich, and without batting an eye he mentioned Marion Edwyn Harrison, the attorney for Free Congress Foundation. He told us he would call Marion and recommend us to him. Over the years Marion Edwyn Harrison has taken very good care of American Life League, advising us, guiding us and protecting us.

It took a few months to work out all the details of starting ALL, and getting the corporate documents needed for IRS approval. I stayed home during that time, helping Paul with LAPAC, caring for the children, and developing ideas for *ALL About Issues*, our organization's newsletter. I wrote the newsletter on an electric typewriter and distributed it using LAPAC's copier and addressograph machine. *ALL About Issues* began as a four-page newsletter printed on white paper in green ink. Measured against today's ALL flagship publication, *Celebrate Life*, those first issues of *ALL About Issues* were amateurish; but the publication was well received and widely distributed throughout the pro-life movement.

Even though *ALL About Issues* began as my brainchild, the concept of reporting the news of the movement was no accident. There had never been anything like it for grassroots people to use, nor had there ever been a magazine focused entirely on personhood.

A few historical landmarks set this magazine apart from all the rest. In 1982 we charted the connections between all those facets of corporate America that contribute to and provide credibility for the pro-death establishment. We presented this material in a format that was easily copied, and it showed up everywhere.

We successfully brought God into the abortion debate and exposed secular humanism—the religion of self. Dr. Murray Norris and Father H. Vernon Sattler, C.Ss.R., helped us formulate articles that made this deceptive mindset easy to understand. They instructed us on the evils inherent in the *Humanist Manifesto* and the theories that underpin the religion of secular humanism.

The magazine hit the difficult questions with factual evidence and human-interest aspects, making it appealing not only to full-time pro-life activists, but also to average people.

I can remember when we first reported on Julie Makimaa, whose mother was violently raped and subsequently gave birth to Julie. The letters poured in from people across the country who never knew that women who had been raped ever kept their babies. Most of them could not have understood why until they read that story.

We published family stories about couples who adopt the hard-to-place babies and the older children often deemed "unwanted."

~

I wound up spending a fair amount of time working through some personal struggles. My last months at NRLC, and my eventual decision to leave, had been very hard on me. Sometimes I felt anger. Sometimes I felt self-pity. Most of the time I felt confusion. I never questioned whether I had done the right thing, but I had to deal with a lot of emotional turmoil. Finally I decided that there was simply nothing I could do about what had happened—but with God's grace, there was a great deal I could do to help other pro-life people become better spokesmen for the Lord in the battle to stop the slaughter of the innocents.

By October, we were ready for our first fund-raising effort. We had to start from scratch. The Viguerie company obtained names of people they thought might be pro-life and sent letters to them, describing our new organization and asking them to support it. It was slow going for a while. In those days, being the director of ALL meant that I was the one who counted the money, wrote the thank-you letters, and answered the phone calls. I was the only "staff" we had.

I must say our children were quite pleased with this whole turn of events, because they got to have Mom at home all the time. I liked it, too. I knew the kids were at an age at which it was important for me to be there for them, and now I was able to do that. The kids grew in their pro-life convictions, too. Even Christy, at the tender age of five, knew that abortion killed babies and was quick to say so to anyone who looked as though he needed to be told.

By the following spring—March 1980—American Life Lobby had grown to a point where it could hire two part-time staffers.

This was when I really began to appreciate our community of Stafford, Virginia. We found people who were capable, committed and more interested in saving babies than in making money (which was fortunate, since we couldn't afford to pay much).

One particular woman, Scarlett Clark, stood on my doorstep, and said to me, "I read your ad in the *Windjammer* newsletter, and do not know what I can do to help you, but would like to interview for a part-time position with ALL." Now, 22 years later, Scarlett is a member of the board of directors and the director of human resources at American Life League. She is one of the most amazing women I have ever had the privilege of knowing. She certainly has made an enormous difference in the way ALL operates.

Since the circulation of *ALL About Issues* was growing, we decided to publish it in a newspaper format once a month. It has always been my philosophy that the best thing I could do to help save the babies was to arm others with the facts and documentation they needed to be effective in the field. Even in those early days, *ALL About Issues* was a valuable asset.

Working on ALL About Issues, the organization's newsletter, in its infancy.

Reviewing ALL About Issues in 1980 with editor Edwin Elliot, Jr.

~

My own thinking about pro-life work went through an important change at this time as well. To be sure, I believed that God was guiding me. I often thought back on the extraordinary events of March 1979, when my time with NRLC ended and my time with ALL started on the same afternoon. It was as though the Lord simply picked me up from the ashes, dusted me off and set me on a new path. I had no thought of leading a group, speaking in public or any of the other astonishing things that were about to come my way. All I knew was that I had to be a better wife and mother, and I had to leave NRLC.

I did know that no single person, no single group and no single political party was going to stop the killing. God, and God alone, would end this horrible crime.

I was finally beginning to learn that we must trust in the Lord rather than in our own pitifully weak resources. We cannot change minds, soften hardened hearts or prick the conscience of a nation—but our Lord can do all these things if we trust in Him. I was beginning to learn that I really wasn't such a smart cookie after all. But the Lord was willing to use me anyway.

Chapter Eleven

We Will Never Forget You

~

1980–1981

*Praised be God, the Father of our Lord
Jesus Christ, the Father of mercies, and
the God of all consolation. He comforts us
in all our afflictions and thus enables us to
comfort those who are in trouble, with the
same consolation we received from him.*
                            —2 Corinthians 1:3–4

We all knew that my mother's condition was steadily deteriorating. I called her as often as I could. My father told me of her diminishing ability to do such simple things as pick up a cup of coffee.

We had already had one crisis with Mama. In 1976, at the height of the chaotic time when I was working 12-hour days at NRLC, I'd had to make two emergency trips to California to be with her. She had pulled through, however, and had been able to spend Christmas with us that year. We couldn't have known it was the last trip she would ever take.

Now, in the summer of 1980, Paul and I loaded up the children and made the trek to Los Angeles, wondering whether it would be our last visit with Mama. The visit went extraordinarily well. Though Mama couldn't move without assistance, she was a joy to be with, and the kids really loved just being with her, talking to her and getting to know her.

We had been back home only a few weeks when Daddy had a heart attack. Back to California I went. The doctors performed quadruple bypass surgery. My sisters and I split the time caring for Mama, and then for Daddy as well when he left the hospital. It soon became clear that Daddy was going to be fine, but that Mama's suffering was only going to get worse. I went back home with a heavy heart.

I decided to put my active pro-life work on the shelf for several weeks so I could devote the holidays to family concerns. Paul and I decided I should go back to California for Thanksgiving.

~

LAPAC had just finished a very successful pre-election "Death Valley Walk." This walk focused attention on the need for prayer and fasting, offered for the election of true pro-life candidates. Thirty pro-lifers joined Paul on a walk that took them from Scotty's Castle, Nevada, to downtown Las Vegas. It was a 100-mile journey—99 miles of grueling desert plus one mile of the Las Vegas strip. But every single participant was pleased to have been part of this historic event—blisters and all.

The walk, which was designed to focus attention on the power of God as the only source of true victory, resonated with everyone who heard about it. Walking across Death Valley for the babies became the theme of many Paul Brown speeches. LAPAC's leadership inspired many to work for truth rather than political "realities" which are often at odds with pro-life principle.

We had much to be thankful for. Our own family was stable. ALL was off to a good start. Paul had founded a management consulting firm in addition to LAPAC, which was also flourishing. The temporary absence of one housewife from the pro-life scene was obviously not going to make a decisive difference. The opportunity to be with my parents again for Thanksgiving turkey was a blessing beyond measure.

$\sim$

One morning I received the phone call I had been dreading for so long. Daddy called to tell me that Mama was gravely ill and that I had better come at once if I wanted to see her alive one last time. Paul immediately called the airline, helped me pack, and drove me to the airport. My brother-in-law met me at the other end and took me straight to my parents' home. I dropped my luggage in a heap inside the front door and went immediately to my mother's bedside.

We talked for about 15 minutes. I still remember her smile and the sparkle in her beautiful brown eyes as she told me she was ready to die. She only hoped that God would forgive her for the many times she had blamed Him for her poor health.

My mother was bedridden by 1980, but loved being with her grandchildren. Back: Mama, Joanna, Kimberly, Christy. Front: Cathy, Dana and Hugh.

At 4:30 the next morning, Daddy woke me up to tell me that Mama had just passed away.

The rest of the day was a blur, handling the countless details of arranging the funeral. I couldn't help but marvel at my step-father. For 10 years he had cared for Mama, and been at her side every minute he was not at work or asleep. He made sure he came home for lunch each day to check on her. No matter what was on his mind, no matter how tired he may have been, no matter how much he might have preferred taking a break, he was always there for Mama. Daddy brought the words of St. Paul to life for me: "He comforts us in all our afflictions and thus enables us to comfort those who are in trouble, with the same consolation we received from him." Daddy has always been for me the embodiment of the true compassion we are meant to show to one another.

After the funeral I hugged Daddy one last time before board-ing the plane to go home. I wept all the way home from Los Angeles. I had lost my closest friend in the world. But I also felt relieved, knowing that Mama was at peace, without pain, and in the presence of the God she loved so dearly.

$$\sim$$

In the meantime, pro-life work was enveloping our house-hold like a giant squid. ALL now had six employees, all of whom worked in our previously unfinished basement, which Paul had had to finish just to provide some modest office space. By the end of 1980 we had more than 35,000 names on our mailing list, and the amount of work was growing just as rapidly—mail to open, requests to answer, letters to write, resource materials to compile. We finally had sufficient funds to open a small office in Washington, where we could be at the heart of the battle.

In March 1981—the month Mama died—we added two more staff members. There was no more room in the basement, so we put them to work in the dining room upstairs. Paul decid-ed that was the last straw. When things got to the point where the children felt like intruders in their own home, he said, it was time to send the pro-life movement packing. So Paul bought an old, run-down building, which became ALL's new headquarters. In September we moved again, into a completely refurbished office building with space for a computer room and proper offices for the staff. Pro-life groups that had once doubted our credibility were beginning to accept the new kid on the block.

That newly won clout quickly became important to us. In October, we tackled something called the Hatch Amendment. This proposed Constitutional amendment, which was endorsed by some pro-life groups, would have said that the right to an abortion was not guaranteed in the Constitution and that states could decide whether to allow, regulate or outlaw abortion.

ALL could not accept such an amendment. The reason seemed simple enough to us—if the Constitution stipulated that a state could prohibit, regulate or permit abortion for any reason, the basic fact of personhood would be lost for all time. If direct killing of innocent persons is not a crime—in every case—then no innocent person is safe. In essence the Hatch Amendment proposed that abortion could be an acceptable option. If that was the best the pro-life movement could do, then it was high time we all packed our bags and left Washington.

We got into a real battle of words with those groups supporting Hatch and his amendment. In the process we invited

*1981:
American Life
Lobby presents
Senator Jesse
Helms with the
Hero of the
Year Award.*

legal scholars like Professor John Baker to prepare talking points for us, to write papers and to testify against the proposal.

A couple of odd things happened during this battle. At one point, as I stood in an elevator with Senator Orrin Hatch, he exclaimed to one of his aides: "This is Judie Brown. She says she is pro-life, but she opposes my amendment. Obviously, she is wrong." I never did figure out what that meant, though Senator Hatch never forgave us for what he perceived as our disruptive activities. Though he never addressed any of our concerns, he made it perfectly clear that he was the most credible Constitutional authority.

When we discussed this with Professor Charles Rice, the leading Constitutional authority on personhood, he smiled and explained that we were naive. Clearly, he said, we had failed to comprehend the obvious. Professor Rice explained that if those in the Republican Party who were pushing for the Hatch Amendment succeeded, they would never again have to take up the question of abortion, and in the process, their goal of avoiding personhood would be achieved. They could then argue that they had done a noble, pro-life duty, even while understanding that the Hatch Amendment permitted abortion to continue unabated if the states wished to allow it. Professor Rice acutely observed that not having to defend the preborn child ever again was really the foundation upon which the Hatch Amendment tactical plan had been laid.

We could not take this lying down. We argued, we debated, we testified, we prayed, we fasted, and in the end we defeated the Hatch Amendment.

The battle over the Hatch Amendment caused a deep division in the pro-life movement, leaving two distinct camps with two distinct ways of politically dealing with abortion. One camp said that "something was better than nothing" and agreed that regulating or limiting the abortion of babies was a worthy goal. On the other hand, ALL was totally unwilling to approve or endorse any proposal that accepts abortion as valid. If the pro-life movement ever argued that each state legislature could regulate, permit or ban abortion, then we were literally saying that there are situations when a lawmaker can allow the direct killing of an innocent child. Such a premise is ludicrous. If some babies are expendable, then all are in danger of death. Every human being is precious and must be protected from the moment of conception.

∾

During the summer of 1981, Father Paul Marx, O.S.B., the founder of Human Life Center in Collegeville, Minnesota, faced unbearable internal conflicts within his organization. There was a concerted effort to remove him from leadership. In desperation, Father Marx came to live with our family for a few weeks as he decided what to do. Our children were amazed by Father Marx, who never stopped teaching the pro-life message and was particularly fond of sharing his wisdom with them. They were young at the time, but eager to soak up the pearls he shared.

By the end of the year Paul had helped Father Marx found Human Life International. It was at our dinner table one evening that Paul recommended the name to Father Marx, who loved it immediately. Shortly after that Father Marx moved to Washington to open the first HLI headquarters. As things turned out, in the Lord's plan, that first HLI office was located in the little office that a growing ALL was vacating.

Chapter Twelve

True Vocation

1982–1983

Let hearts rejoice who search for the Lord.
Seek the Lord and his strength; seek
always the face of the Lord.

—Psalm 105:3–4

The year 1982 was one of transition for our pro-life work and for me personally. It began with the annual get-together of pro-life leaders with President Ronald Reagan on the anniversary of the *Roe v. Wade* decision. President Reagan really invigorated us with his strongly expressed desire that abortion be stopped.

~

But political action in the pro-life arena was weakening, diluted by the compromising attitudes of so many leaders and groups. It had reached the point where politicians could get away with adopting the "pro-life" label merely by opposing tax-payer funding of abortion, without expressing any commitment to the absolute personhood of the preborn child.

Paul decided the time had come to step down from his position with the Life Amendment Political Action Committee. This was due in part to his frustration over the state of affairs in the political action realm and in part to a desire to separate LAPAC from ALL in people's minds. In reality, the only link between the two groups was the fact that their respective directors happened to be married to each other, but people understandably tended to assume they were all part of the same organization. Paul hosted the second, and last, Death Valley Walk in October of 1982 and handed over the reins of LAPAC to others. He focused his

Left: I pose with presidential candidate Ronald Reagan during a political gathering in early 1980.

Right: I accept Pro-Life Action League Award from league director Joe Scheidler, 1982.

energies on his consulting business and on serving as my chief advisor at ALL.

Our work was continuing to expand, both in size and influence. American Life League now had more than 75,000 supporters. *ALL About Issues* had become a 48-page magazine circulated to more than 100,000 people in more than 30 countries. Though we had not stopped legalized abortion, we had helped save babies by equipping people to work against abortion from the pulpit, in the classroom, and on the sidewalks in front of abortion clinics.

It was in the pages of *ALL About Issues* that the grisly baby body parts industry was first exposed in 1982. Olga Fairfax wrote an article, "101 Uses for a Dead Baby," that created quite a stir. It seemed the entire world was focused on proving her "claims" were false. But no one was ever able to debunk one single sentence of that article. Shortly after this article appeared, investigative reporter Suzanne Rini's book, *Beyond Abortion*, corroborated all that Fairfax had written. The sad reality is that the industry exposed in 1982 continues to thrive.

Just as things were going so well, Ash Wednesday arrived— and with it a lawsuit. It involved a contractual dispute between American Life Lobby and the company that was handling our direct-mail fundraising. Frankly, we had grown so fast, and with

I testify against taxpayer funding for Planned Parenthood before an apathetic Congressional committee, 1983.

so little experience at running a big organization, that we had trouble staying on top of endless details. We were eventually able to settle the lawsuit amicably, and in a way that made us stronger as an organization. But when the suit was filed, it was a real blow. It had the capacity to cripple American Life Lobby and to threaten the effectiveness of American Life League.

I did two things that Ash Wednesday in response to the lawsuit. First, I went to our lawyer. Second, I went to Mass. I felt as though this latest crisis was going to drive me over the edge unless something major happened. As it turned out, something major did happen. The Lord used the situation to bring me, at long last, fully to Himself.

It didn't start out all that "spiritual." I prayed vigorously that the Lord would help us deal with the lawsuit, and in a way that would enable both American Life Lobby and American Life League to remain in operation. I told him that if he would help us out of the mess we were in, I would lose 100 pounds.

I know, I know. You're not supposed to make deals with God. But I didn't really think of it that way at the time. I simply had problems that were too big for me to handle, and I was asking the Lord to take charge of everything in my life.

I set about reviewing every aspect of my life, beginning with my commitment to my vocation of being a wife and mother. I had been so moody and irritable with Paul and the kids, it was a wonder they hadn't strung me up long before. A number of things became clear to me.

First, as someone who had become accustomed to being introduced as a "pro-life leader," I really thought I had all the answers and that victory would come about because of my efforts. Wrong!

I felt that my husband and children should accept the fact that pro-life work demanded most of my waking hours, including evenings and weekends, and that housekeeping, cooking, and laundry were not matters that needed my concern. Wrong!

When I did prepare meals, I felt we shouldn't let anything go to waste, and that every morsel of food not consumed by someone else had to be consumed by me. Wrong!

I felt that being in church with God once a week should be enough for anyone. Wrong—at least for me.

One by one, the scales fell from my eyes. It was suddenly obvious that I had to make immense changes in my life if I were ever to realize my hopes and dreams—especially my desire to one day see my mother again in heaven. I felt that the words of the book of Revelation applied to me:

> *Wake up, and strengthen what remains before it dies. I find that the sum of your deeds is less than complete in the eyes of my God.*
>
> *I know your deeds; I know you are neither hot nor cold. How I wish you were one or the other—hot or cold. But because you are lukewarm, neither hot nor cold, I will spew you out of my mouth.*
>
> *—Revelation 3:2, 15–16*

~

It was all too true. Without a doubt I was headed straight for the lukewarm spirituality that is so offensive to our Lord. I had become a couch potato in God's vineyard. That Lent I became acquainted, as never before, with my own need and my own faith—and with the need to nurture that faith more than once a week on Sunday mornings.

It was a slow, painful process. It took almost a year to get down to my desired weight of 145 pounds. But with the Lord's help, I made it. I never went to a diet counselor or even a doctor. I just began taking vitamins, cooking for a family and eating for a sparrow. What a novel experience, leaving food on the plate. When I stopped eating fat, the fat went away. Gradually I shrank from a size 24 to a size 10. My kids—now ages 13, 11 and 8— really noticed the change. The day Hugh said to me, "Mom, you really look great," was one of the brightest days of my life.

The lawsuit that had started on Ash Wednesday ended, interestingly enough, on Good Friday, when our lawyer called to say that an amicable resolution had been reached. The fund-raising company took a hands-on approach to helping the lobby retire a debt that had seemed unmanageable, and the lobby, in turn, became a fiscally sound organization. Thus we turned a major corner in our ability to serve those who were looking for a pro-life group that would lead, not wait; that would fight, not stand still; that would hold the line for the babies, not cut deals.

Paul never wavered in his support through all this. People sometimes say that marriage is a 50–50 proposition, but they couldn't be more wrong. There have been times when our marriage was a 100–0 proposition, in one direction or the other. Through each of these periods our love grew stronger, our faith grew deeper, and our ability to withstand whatever was thrown in our way became greater.

It is impossible to continue in pro-life work without strong family support and constant re-examination of priorities. I always tell people that God gave me one vocation—to be a good wife and mother. When I falter in that vocation, then nothing else in my life will bear good fruit. To be pro-life means to be pro-family first, and that commitment must take tangible form in the way we live our daily lives.

The events of this hectic year finally brought me to my knees—literally—at daily Mass. Receiving the Eucharist has become the cornerstone of my relationship with the Lord, and as a consequence, with every aspect of my life.

The Brown family, Christmas 1983.

It humbles me that I had to sink so low before I could realize how distorted were my priorities and how great was my need for the Lord. It was, of course, nothing more than what my parents had tried to teach me—and what the Lord had been trying to get across to me.

$\sim$

I received a call from a dear friend of mine, Daniel Overduin, who had served on the Alternatives to Abortion International Board with me. He was the author of the still widely read book, *Babies Made in Glass*, which exposes the fallacy of in vitro fertilization technology. Daniel suggested that we put together an international organization of pro-life leaders to meet annually and discuss our mutual concerns, goals and aspirations. I was intrigued with this, and immediately asked for guidance from our spiritual director, Father Denis O'Brien, who concurred.

From that initial conversation, Protect Life in All Nations was formed, first on paper, and then with a strategic planning meeting held in Ireland that September. Many of those who attended, including Daniel Overduin, were of like mind—even Dr. C. Everett Koop, who gave us many excellent suggestions. Some of the others who attended were Paul Brown, Dr. John Willke, Dr. Philippe Schepens, Dr. Karl F. Gunning and Dr. Herbert Ratner. We had gathered together a remarkable group of people who wished to focus on the plans and goals of ending abortion around the world.

The next year, 1983, Paul flew to Kenya, to arrange for a second meeting incorporating the thoughts we had formulated in Ireland. He met with Father Maurice Lwanga, assistant to the bishops of Kenya, and the second meeting took place later that same year. Clearly, the ideas for PLAN were widely accepted, and the concept grew. I now realize that these early days were the foundation we needed for World Life League, the current international division of American Life League.

Chapter Thirteen

ALL Advances, the White House Retreats

~

1983–1985

Do not grow lazy, but imitate those who,
through faith and patience, are inheriting
the promises.

—Hebrews 6:12

American Life League's influence began to extend farther and farther. In late 1983 we helped sponsor an international pro-life congress in Rome. This gathering was the result of meetings throughout the previous year among pro-life leaders from various organizations, who agreed that the relationship of birth control to abortion needed to be addressed more forcefully.

The congress was a real watershed. Speakers came to Rome from around the world—as far away as Africa and China—and told story after story of how officials from the United States Agency for International Development had vigorously advanced the pro-abortion, pro-death agenda in their countries. Tapes of these presentations were sent to officials in the Reagan administration. We were certain they would make an impact there.

But we were wrong. We never heard a word from anyone in the administration about the tapes or the horror stories they contained. The silence was deafening. Was this alleged pro-life White House starting to weaken? Was our pro-life president revealing feet of clay?

Politics, we were to discover, could have strange effects on people.

～

It was 1984—an election year. The year had long since been immortalized by George Orwell's famous novel about a society where everything was turned upside down—weakness was strength, truth was fiction, black was white. It was in 1984 that we began to see pro-life dollars funding the re-election campaigns of several pro-abortion senators simply because they were Republicans, as it was considered important in some quarters to retain a Republican majority in the Senate. No one ever seemed to stop and ask why a Republican majority was so important if the Republicans in question were not willing to support measures that would protect preborn babies. In fact, the question was never even posed.

It was also in 1984 that a major international meeting in Mexico City addressed world population. The aim was to help disadvantaged nations address the economic problems caused by "overpopulation."

It didn't take a genius to figure out the agenda of many of these policy makers. They pressed for greater use of birth control and abortion, rather than addressing the real needs of families. We needed a way to influence the meeting directly. We no longer felt we could trust the White House, where the retreat from pro-life principle was now almost complete.

Members of our staff collected the material that would best substantiate the known fact that population control was not only a threat to families but also a failure that caused misery all over the world. Professor Julian Simon, who traveled to the Mexico City conference as an expert, agreed with our position and made some valuable recommendations to us. We needed to send someone to Mexico City who would get the job done on our behalf and not wind up playing footsie with the enemy. He had become quite familiar with Paul and me due to our commitment to opposing population control, and he immediately recommended Paul Brown as our emissary.

Senator James Buckley, a strong pro-lifer who was part of the U.S. delegation, helped Paul and Julian get research material into the right hands. During one lobbying session, Professor Simon spoke with a United Nations statistician. Julian pointed out how erroneous the U.N. statistics were, and the official replied, "Julian, I know that. But this is my job and I publish what my bosses want to hear, regardless of whether it is right or wrong." So much for the truth at the U.N.

Ultimately, Senator Buckley, speaking on behalf of the Reagan Administration in Mexico City, announced that the United States would deny financial support to any government that used coercive family-planning methods or that utilized abortion as a means of birth control. Mild as that policy was, it sent shivers down the spines of the pro-death groups—which was precisely our intent. United Nations operatives were hopping mad, not only with the Reagan Administration decision, but also with Julian Simon and Paul Brown.

Julian Simon passed away in 1998. But his work survives, even now, as the best and most credible in the field. In fact, when the *Washington Post Book World* reviewed his book, *Ultimate Resource II*, the reviewer said the book was "the most powerful challenge to be mounted against the principles of popular environmentalism in the last fifteen years."

Professor Julian Simon frequently offered a reward to anyone who could disprove the facts in his many books. Never was he placed in the position of having to pay that reward.

～

In September 1984 our international organization, Protect Life in All Nations, met in Rome. During that meeting a member of our board was invited to attend a private Papal Mass. But I knew that I could not attend because we had brought our three children along and had already scheduled our departure from Rome to coincide with school schedules. So I asked Gabrielle Avery, one of ALL's founders, if she would represent American Life League at the Mass. I also asked her if she would present Pope John Paul II with a 14-karat-gold set of Precious Feet, as a token of the American pro-life movement's gratitude to him for his strong leadership in defense of life.

Gabrielle was so overcome that she spoke of that Mass and her presence in the same chapel with the Holy Father as though she had already arrived in heaven. Gabrielle was always there with a smile, a willing hand and was in no small measure a guiding light in the many struggles ALL had to deal with in our early years.

～

The annual meeting of pro-life leaders and the president in 1985 changed my attitude toward politics and politicians forever.

The invitation came from the White House liaison for social policy affairs. The invitation was to both Paul and me—me because of ALL, Paul because of his political acumen and his experience with LAPAC.

These kinds of meetings with the president are always carefully orchestrated, almost scripted. Those invited to the meeting propose topics to be discussed, which are assembled into a briefing book. The president's staff reviews the contents of the book with him, so that he will be able to engage the issues without spending a lot of time on background information. The participants, for their part, decide ahead of time who will address which segment of the book, to avoid duplication of effort and to make sure all the main points get covered.

When the White House representative asked me what I wanted to address, I responded immediately. We were facing a new threat, I told him—a drug called RU-486, which was designed to induce "do-it-yourself" abortions through the 10th week of pregnancy. It was imperative, I said, to stop federally funded research on RU-486, and to deny Food and Drug Administration approval of this drug. I felt that the president could play an important role in carrying out these tasks.

I was astonished by the man's response. RU-486 was not in the briefing book, he said, so the president would not be prepared to discuss it fruitfully. Therefore, I was not to bring it up at the meeting under any circumstances. After all, he said, we did not want to embarrass the president.

It seemed to me that if the president was unaware of what RU-486 was, and also unaware of the fact that his own government was sponsoring its development, then he needed to know about it, whether it was embarrassing or not. Most of the embarrassment, I suspected, would be on the part of those White House aides who seemed to be keeping the president in the dark on this crucial matter.

When my turn came to speak at the meeting, I told President Reagan about the RU-486 "death pill." I handed him copies of research grants that the government was sponsoring, and pleaded with him to stop the funding. He seemed amazed, though not particularly embarrassed. He asked me several questions and assured me that action would be forthcoming.

Paul also launched into a topic that wasn't "in the book." He told the stories of several pro-life activists who had been given extraordinarily harsh jail sentences for a variety of alleged offenses. Couldn't the White House review these cases, he asked, and look into getting the sentences reduced or even remitted on a case-by-case basis? The president said he was unaware that such cases existed and promised to look into the matter.

The record shows that the White House did nothing to block RU-486 research funding, and next to nothing about the pro-lifers who had been so unjustly treated by the courts. It was the clearest indication to date of the true colors of the White House. While President Reagan was committed to a pro-life America, he was surrounded by staffers and advisors who either did not share his position or considered it less than a priority. Indeed, we later learned that there were people in the administration who worked without ceasing to block action on any of our suggestions. I was simply too naive to realize it at the time.

The only concrete result of that particular afternoon was that Paul and I were told we would never be invited back to the White House again. We felt vindicated, somehow. Had we gone along with the "briefing book game" and remained silent, we would have been untrue to our principles, to the babies and to God. If we were going to offend someone, we decided, then White House staffers were the ones to offend, not the Lord.

When we explained these events to the kids, all three of them agreed that Mom and Dad had done the right thing. Isn't it ironic that children see the facts without anyone having to wrap them in nice words or sound bites? They instinctively

know when someone is trying to pull the wool over their eyes. If only adults could be so honest!

~

ALL's growing influence meant that grassroots pro-lifers began seeking our help to fight Planned Parenthood's sex education programs. These programs were steeped in moral relativism and lacked all respect for parental authority. In fact, parental authority was being undermined at every turn by the classroom sex gurus.

Yet the sad fact was that pro-life parents who held these concerns had absolutely nowhere to go. The one guide they could use, but few knew of, was a remarkable book written by a leading pro-life physician. The book was *A Very Grimm Fairy Tale*, and the author was James H. Ford, M.D., a member of the California Medical Association who had been battling the CMA's involvement in sex "instruction" since the late 1960s. Dr. Ford served on our board in the 1980s. He was quick to respond to

Above: Meeting with President Reagan, 1985.

Left: Article appearing in The Washington Times on January 20, 1984.

the growing menace of Planned Parenthood and immediately led us in the proper direction.

Dr. Ford simply said to me: "Judie, you have three children. What would you do if Hugh, for example, came home and told you that he had learned in school that having sexual relations with a girl was really quite all right as long as he took steps to protect himself?" My mouth dropped open. Hugh was in the eighth grade and 14 years old at the time. Frankly, had he ever said something like that to me, I would have given him quite a lecture—that is after I picked myself up off the ground. I knew, without a doubt, that American Life League had to make a total commitment to this fight and take no prisoners in the process.

Guided by the leadership of our board, we followed Dr. Ford's lead and described sex "education" as sex "instruction." We published a series of analyses in our magazine, taking the position that opposing permissive sex instruction meant opposing all methods of birth control. The link was obvious. It was increasingly evident that the pro-abortion forces despised the very idea of pro-lifers pointing out that the contraceptive mentality was the breeding ground for abortion. Every time we pointed out that sex instruction denied parental authority, you could watch the hairs on the back of our opponents' necks stand right up in fright. We were winning the battle by teaching the truth.

As ALL became known for our "strident" defense of purity, I became popular with the media. They needed someone to oppose the spate of proposals from pro-abortion groups to place birth control ads on television. This new twist played right into our opponents' overall game plan to brainwash young people in the classroom, in magazines and on the tube.

I recall numerous pro-lifers who called me to find out how to respond effectively to such ridiculous issues as whether or not TV ads for birth control were appropriate. Within a few months, the furor died down; pro-lifers succeeded—at least for a time. The ads never aired that year, but Planned Parenthood continued undaunted.

I remember one particular televised encounter I had early in 1984 with Planned Parenthood president Faye Wattleton. Dr.

Ford had thoroughly briefed me on the standard rhetoric used by such puppets of the Culture of Death, and I found Faye quite willing to "debate" the differences between innocence as a virtue and promiscuity as a sin. Her comments made my job quite easy and several people felt I had handily won the debate. I knew that it was not I, but the Holy Spirit speaking through me, who captured whatever victory was achieved that day.

∼

PLAN hosted a fourth gathering in Scotland. This time we were treated to a visit from Wanda Paltawska, M.D., of Poland, a friend of Pope John Paul II. We also hosted a member of the Pontifical Council for the Family, Mario Zivkovic. PLAN was growing and helping the international pro-life community speak with a steady and very principled voice.

I was constantly amazed and humbled to realize that we are all interconnected as a worldwide body of people who want nothing more than to be Christ's arms and legs.

Chapter Fourteen

If I Should Die Before I Wake

1985

*"Peace" is my farewell to you, my peace is
my gift to you; I do not give it to you as
the world gives peace. Do not be distressed
or fearful.*

—John 14:27

Some of ALL's greatest advances came in 1985, as well as of one of the most harrowing crises of my life.

The nature of the pro-life struggle began to shift with the advent of a new concept in "education." The idea was labeled "school-based clinics," or SBCs. The scheme seemed simple— clinics located inside elementary schools, middle schools and high schools, where children could receive needed medical attention and counseling free of charge. Sounds great, doesn't it?

But we began to smell a rat when we saw the names of the people who were advocating SBCs. There was Douglas Kirby, a former official of the federal Centers for Disease Control in Atlanta, who had long ago established himself as a leading advocate of expanded sex "education" in the schools. He was also a proponent of providing birth control advice (and products), as well as abortion referrals, either in the schools or in clinics located nearby. His extensive relationship with the likes of Planned Parenthood made that rat appear larger than life.

The second player who caught our attention was Joy Dryfoos, a researcher whose articles appeared regularly in Family Planning Perspectives, published by the Alan Guttmacher Institute, which is the research arm of Planned Parenthood. She became very vocal about the "national crisis" of rising teen pregnancy rates, which she not surprisingly attributed to a lack of adequate sex "education" in the schools.

Somehow, with people like this involved, we suspected that SBCs had an agenda beyond treating head colds and upset stomachs. We were right. As the SBC movement picked up speed, it became clear that the primary purpose of the clinics was to advance the pro-birth control, pro-abortion agenda. There are documented cases of students going into such clinics for something as simple as an aspirin, only to be asked to complete a survey of intimate questions about sexual behavior. The follow-up to this, of course, is an offer of birth control and abortion referral services to any students who might "need" them.

Outstanding pro-life experts who had really made a niche for themselves in this specific arena of government-funded birth control programs approached us. Mary Kempf of St. Louis had complete dossiers on Kirby, Dryfoos and others. She said there was no doubt that the SBC movement was going to get government support and grow quickly. Pastor Hiram Crawford of Chicago, who led a unique African-American pro-life, pro-family group, said he would work to stop these clinics from "infecting" inner-city Chicago schools. Pat Riehle in California began speaking to church groups, legislative sessions and anywhere people would gather to listen to the facts. Nancy Czierwiec put together enormous meetings in the Chicago suburbs. Each of these grassroots heroes, along with countless others, sought American Life League's help so that SBCs would not become hazardous to the health of our children.

When we went into battle against school-based clinics, we started with a solid reputation for our research and expertise. But even more importantly, through an organization we collaborated in founding, the American Family Defense Coalition, we were able to assist grassroots pro-lifers in effectively battling the threat to their children. The AFDC effectively took the battlefield where it needed to go at the time: school board meetings.

Of great importance in this latest battle was the handbook our research expert, Robert G. Marshall, carefully put together. We naively believed that the documented facts were the only tool needed for parents to make their voices heard and their message heeded. How could anyone argue with the facts?

Many television and radio interviews and debates resulted. I've always been grateful to the Lord for the way we were able to spearhead what became a broad-based struggle to stop the spread of this new assault on our children.

~

I was called on once again to debate Faye Wattleton, the president of Planned Parenthood. But this time it was to be on *Donahue*. I was so nervous about the broadcast that I nearly became ill. The morning of the show, I went to Mass at St. Patrick's Cathedral in New York. I really wasn't concerned so much about embarrassing myself, but I didn't want to say anything that would betray my faith and reliance on the Lord.

I took it as a sign of special favor from the Lord that Cardinal John O'Connor himself was the celebrant that morning. He was my hero. He remains an extraordinary example of precisely what the Lord's shepherds are called to be. The point of his brief homily that "Donahue morning" was that when we are in distress, we must give our problems to God with faith and hope. I knew this was the Lord's way of telling me not to worry.

As Faye Wattleton and I, along with a pro-abortion physician, sat down to be Phil Donahue's guests for an hour, an aura of peace surrounded me. The butterflies died down, the knees stopped knocking, and I said a very quick Hail Mary as Phil responded to the camera lights and introduced us.

Faye and I debated RU-486, with her side counting Phil and the doctor as allies. It was astonishing how candid and matter-of-fact Ms. Wattleton was in describing how the chemical could kill preborn babies through the 10th week of pregnancy, and how energetic the audience was in its appreciation of such efficient killing.

It seemed to me that Phil Donahue gave me more than my share of the time, perhaps hoping to balance things out a bit. Still, when I expressed support for chastity outside of marriage and fidelity in marriage, I thought Phil would have to have his jaw scraped off the floor. In fact, a young lady in the audience

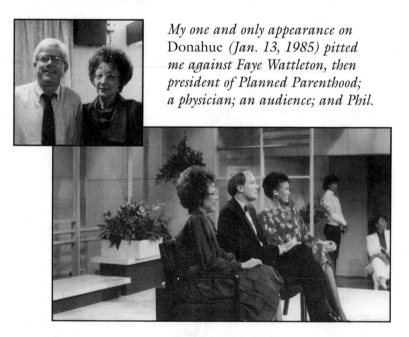

My one and only appearance on Donahue *(Jan. 13, 1985) pitted me against Faye Wattleton, then president of Planned Parenthood; a physician; an audience; and Phil.*

stood up and ridiculed me for not understanding that having sex is something everyone does, and I should know better than to think that young people would "save themselves" for marriage. She scowled, she raised her voice, and the crowd went wild in agreement with her view. But Phil expressed dismay at their behavior, and said that they should at least hear me out. I told the audience that in the early 1960s there were but five strains of venereal disease, and that in 1985 there were 35. I told them where they could look to substantiate these numbers. I explained that most strains were not curable, and that often the young women who acquired these diseases were never able to bear children. All of a sudden the audience was listening a little closer and laughing a little less.

Then, I moved on to the facts about RU-486 and the reality of how each member of the audience was there that day because their mothers had chosen life rather than death for them. Not all were happy to hear this, but I could tell that some of them were at least thinking rather than jawboning to get their face on camera. Through it all, including the catcalls and the screaming, I felt utterly calm and at peace. I knew the Holy Spirit was there, protecting me and guiding my tongue.

~

In July, my world seemed to come crashing down around me. Following three days of hemorrhaging, my gynecologist told me her examination had indicated a possibly cancerous growth in my left ovary. A radical hysterectomy was necessary, she said, and the sooner the better. She referred me to a group of specialists at Georgetown University Hospital.

This was serious news indeed. There are many kinds of cancer, some more dangerous than others. Ovarian cancer can be one of the most dangerous of all. I went through a battery of tests at Georgetown, all of which confirmed the original diagnosis.

The doctors wanted to operate right away. There was only one problem: Paul and I had finally been able to plan a vacation together—the first one we'd had since our first year of marriage —and we didn't want to miss out on it now. We had planned to cover more than 3,000 miles driving and to be gone about three weeks.

The doctor sat quietly for a moment, then said, "Go ahead. Three weeks won't make that much difference. Either it's already gone too far, or we've caught it in time, or we're just plain wrong about it being cancer in the first place. So don't worry, just have a good time." Paul and I looked at each other and decided that we would have a good time. And we did. It was one of the most memorable and enjoyable trips we ever made.

The day before I went into the hospital, we invited a dear friend and advisor, Father H. Vernon Sattler, C.Ss.R., to come to the house for dinner. Father Sattler had just joined ALL as director of the Castello Institute of Stafford (now known as the American Bioethics Advisory Commission), a think tank we established to study ethical questions. Father Sattler had promised ALL one year of his life, and in retrospect, God gave us the very year in which I would need him the most. I had asked him to say Mass for our family, administer the sacrament of the Anointing of the Sick to me, and talk to the children about how to place their trust in the Lord. It was very hard for the children—now ages 16, 14 and 11—to face the fact that I might die. But it was something I wanted them to be able to deal with in a spiritual way. If I did leave them, I wanted them to have confidence that God had a perfect plan for me, and for them as well.

Above: Recuperating at home after my surgery.

Right: The front cover of The Washington Post *on January 5, 1986.*

The next morning I said goodbye to Paul, in case I didn't get the chance to speak to him later, and assured him that everything would be okay. I learned later that while he sat in the waiting room during my surgery, he happened to pick up an article about the high number of women who die from ovarian cancer. It really tore him up. I was glad to have the opportunity to hear about it and to be able to share with him my philosophy about death. How important it is to be spiritually prepared to die. How fortunate I felt to have had several weeks in which to make those preparations.

As things turned out, I did indeed have cancer. But the operation was a success. All the cancerous cells were removed. I never needed any follow-up radiation or chemotherapy. To this day—praise God—I remain cancer-free.

~

The doctor prescribed six full weeks of bed rest for my recuperation. I complied fully with everything he told me to do—not because I'm such a cooperative person by nature, but because Paul hovered over me like a mother hen, making sure I behaved myself. I was not allowed to get up from the couch for any but the most pressing reasons. You would have thought I was his child, not his wife. But that is the way Paul is, and I am grateful to God for such a husband.

Six weeks to the day after the operation, I met with a reporter from the *Washington Post* who wanted to do a story about me for the paper's Sunday magazine. I had to chuckle at the timing.

On January 22, 1986, the paper arrived with a full-color picture of me on the cover of the magazine and a wonderful story about this woman who traveled around the country speaking about chastity, preborn babies and birth control. Though the writer, Walt Harrington, had the chance to flay me, he wrote a great piece for the babies. He wrote about pro-lifers in a positive way. I hope it affected him, and many of his readers, in some small way, so they can better appreciate the battle we are fighting and the sincerity of our efforts.

Chapter Fifteen

On the Field, in the Courts, at the Polls

~

1986–1988

*Those who love your law have great
peace, and for them there is no
stumbling block.*

—Psalm 119:165

"Hey!" exclaimed my husband. "Did you know that Tommy Herr is one of our donors? How about that? Tommy Herr."

"Yeah, how about that," I answered unenthusiastically. "So who's Tommy Herr?"

So much for my knowledge of professional athletes.

Tommy Herr was the second baseman for the St. Louis Cardinals, renowned for his talent both in the field and at the plate. It also turned out that he was pro-life and that he liked American Life League enough to support us financially.

Learning that Tommy was one of our supporters immediately revitalized an old idea, that we start a group called "Athletes for Life." Another professional baseball player, Chris Speier, had tried to form such a group a few years before, but it had not gotten off the ground for a variety of reasons. Apparently the timing just hadn't been right in the Lord's plan.

But was the timing right now? One of our staff members contacted Tommy, who responded enthusiastically. Tommy was perfect for the leadership role. As chairman of Athletes for Life,

Athletes for Life, begun in 1978 and carried forward in 1985 by American Life League, provides athletes with information and fellowship. Right: Mike Ditka. Below: George Martin, Fr. Kenneth Moore, O.Corm., Wellington Mara, Mark Bavaro.

he enrolled many of his fellow ball players. He also appeared in a number of televised public service announcements, telling the American public the truth about the high failure rate of condoms and the foolproof way to prevent the transmission of AIDS through sexual contact—chastity. He was terrific.

The idea grew from there. Before long Mark Bavaro, the all-pro tight end for the New York Giants, became co-chairman of Athletes for Life and started signing up professional football players as well. He even went to the first Operation Rescue event in New York City as an observer and wound up in a paddy wagon. Athletes for Life has been extremely effective in carrying the pro-life message to the public, especially among young people.

～

Speaking of Operation Rescue, I participated in a rescue that year as well. One of my favorite priests, Father James Buckley, told me he was going to participate and urged me to join him. So one Saturday morning I drove to Fairfax, Virginia, to join a group of rescuers committed to closing down a local abortion clinic.

It was an experience I'll never forget. We were all gathered on the sidewalk when the signal came to move into place in front of the clinic's doors. Everyone around me began moving. I had planned to join them. I lifted my right foot to take a step forward, and then simply got stuck. I can't explain it, but it felt as though my feet were literally riveted to the ground. I tried to move, but I absolutely could not do so. The rescue took place with me standing there, praying my Rosary, still frozen to the sidewalk.

There are many charisms and callings, as Cardinal O'Connor so frequently reminded us, but apparently participating in Operation Rescue was not one of mine. I applaud the valiant efforts of those who literally stand in the way of the slaughter, but it does not appear to be my calling.

The rescue movement, though, influenced ALL in an unexpected and unwelcome way. In 1987, with Operation Rescue rolling across the country like a freight train, the abortion lobby came up with a new legal strategy—taking pro-lifers to court under a law designed to deal with organized crime. The law is called the RICO act, because of its stated goal of stopping "racketeer influenced and corrupt organizations." The abortionists argued that Operation Rescue's orchestrated attempts to close down abortion clinics violated this statute. Even though ALL was not formally aligned with Operation Rescue, we were hit with a RICO lawsuit just the same.

It wasn't until 1989—following a lot of anxiety and a fortune in legal fees—that we were finally free of the case. Nothing really came of it except a couple of years of legal maneuvering by three well-versed attorneys who defended us. Yet the travesty of the RICO act continues. It is appalling that those who kill babies are able to go about their business under the protection of the law, while those who sacrifice so much to intervene on behalf of innocent preborn babies go to jail—as gangsters, no less.

I believe the history books will one day honor these courageous men and women who put their lives on the line for the sake of the babies in an effort to awaken a slumbering nation to the horror of abortion. Such deeds are acts of selfless love, taken not to gain praise or notoriety, but to say with one's heart and soul that every innocent human being deserves to be welcomed, protected and respected.

The founder of the Lambs of Christ, Father Norm Weslin, has told me personally and has preached to thousands that Christ is calling us to do something, and whether we do it or not deter-

1988 took me out to the states for speeches and to America through television interviews in my office.

mines our role in reshaping this society. Some are called to go to jail and some are not. But everyone is called to do something.

My view is that those who pray—for the preborn, for their mothers, and for their killers—are every bit as courageous, and every bit as effective, as those who intervene physically. Each of us has his own gift, and his own calling, from the Lord. God does not expect us to do what He has called others to do, only what He has called us to do. For some this is education, for others it is politics, and for still others it is intercessory prayer. Every action taken is activism, nothing more and nothing less.

Father Denis O'Brien, M.M., frequently reminds me that when it comes to taking credit for anything, it is far better to realize that God is keeping score rather than to worry about getting recognition in the here and now.

∼

As the 1988 presidential election rolled around, American Life Lobby received many letters from supporters, wondering how we planned to work for the Bush campaign and how they could join in. A lot of these people were angry—and more than a few stopped contributing—when we told them that we did not plan to do anything for the Bush campaign.

1988 also took me to Congress to point out the plight of preborn children and their mothers as victims of abortion.

We heard from many people who accused me of being an ostrich who had buried my head in the sand; a couple of people called me a numbskull—and worse. They argued that "Bush was more pro-life" than his opponent, and so I should get a grip and understand that in politics nobody is perfect. I was told that by withholding support from Bush, I was helping pro-aborts take over and the deaths of babies would be on my conscience.

I wrote to each of these lovely people, knowing that I owed them a complete explanation. To my mind the reasons for not supporting Bush were sound and logical.

Our board of directors and our legal and medical advisors were unanimous in their conviction that protection of the child in the womb had to be absolute. Any candidate who wanted to wear the pro-life label had to be unequivocally committed to the principle that all the babies had to be protected, not just some of them. So when George Bush went on record as saying he opposed abortion except in cases of rape, incest, or to save the life of the mother, it was clear that we could not endorse him— even though his opponent, Michael Dukakis, was far worse. If a man could get away with support for some abortion and still be welcomed as a pro-life candidate, then after he attained elective office, his duty to uphold principle was already in the trash heap of political promises.

My response did not resonate with everyone who complained, but a great many of our supporters began to think about the long-term effects of supporting quasi-pro-life candidates, and they agreed with our assessment. Time has borne out the wisdom of our position, which was controversial then, and raises hackles even now.

The state of pro-life political action had been deteriorating for some time, and became especially troublesome in 1988. More and more candidates were trying to endear themselves to the pro-life movement by mouthing weak, ambiguous statements. More and more pro-life people were buying the argument that "something" was better than "nothing." As a result, the pro-life movement's political clout had been severely diluted. ALL's position was clear and uncompromising: we would give no endorsement to any candidate who did not stand four-square for equal protection for all the babies.

The only bright spot of 1988 was Pat Robertson. He campaigned on the truth of what Planned Parenthood really represented. He pointed out that the group's founder, Margaret Sanger, had been a racist. He spoke forthrightly about how abortion was tearing at the heart of our nation. Robertson's comments, however, helped end his bid for the White House. Media attention and attacks on him resulted in his early departure from the campaign.

The result was that, while pro-lifers might have convinced George Bush to adopt a more acceptable position, the establishment Republican wing of the movement found more solace in befriending Bush than in chastising him. Our movement failed to stand firm for the truth. Instead we built a stumbling block and fell over it ourselves.

Our opponents, of course, did not make this mistake. They did not give an inch to anyone. They wanted abortion on demand, right now, period. Their unbending insistence on the woman's "right to choose" easily overcame the pro-life movement's tepid stand of "no killing—except under certain circumstances."

Dr. Bernard Nathanson, the former abortionist who later converted to the pro-life cause, pointed out that the pro-abortion forces have long been able to take advantage of compromise and division among pro-lifers. One of the main strategies of the National Abortion Rights Action League, of which Dr. Nathanson was a founder, was to stand solidly for its demands in the face of division and waffling from the churches and the pro-life groups. In particular, he said, it had taken advantage of division among the Roman Catholic hierarchy, working in various ways to drive the wedge in deeper.

It had worked as early as 1973, and it was still working in 1988. The pro-abortionists held fast to their cardinal principles while we shied away from our own. The tragedy of the strategic "something-is-better-than-nothing" approach is that babies die as a result. I only wish we were more concerned with standing firm for God's truth than with finding acceptance in the halls of secular power.

Chapter Sixteen

Matters of Opinion

~

1989

*I have come in my Father's name, yet you
do not accept me. But let someone come in
his own name and him you will accept.
How can people like you believe, when
you accept praise from one another yet do
not seek the glory that comes from the
One God?*

—John 5:37–38

Christy was the center of my life during 1989.

In most ways, the Brown family was doing great. Hugh was playing football at the University of Maryland, and Cathy had begun her studies at George Mason University. Paul's business had grown and prospered. His plant was now printing most of ALL's publications, and he volunteered his spare time to help us manage ALL's finances. With his expertise we could maximize the value of every penny donated by our 250,000 supporters.

The only cloud on the horizon was Christy. She was ill and no one could figure out the nature of her illness. She suffered severe chest and abdominal pain, which totally debilitated her every time it flared up. We went from doctor to doctor, who put Christy through test after test, only to come back shrugging their shoulders and shaking their heads.

Fortunately, ALL now had a staff in place and my physical presence was not required in the office very much. As long as the telephone system kept operating, I was able to stay home with Christy whenever she needed me. That was a great blessing.

~

In the midst of Christy's troubles, we began to face another dilemma on the pro-life front. It had to do with a Supreme Court case known as *Webster v. Reproductive Health Services*. It was one of the most closely watched abortion-related cases in many years.

William Webster was attorney general for the state of Missouri. That state's restrictions on abortion were among the most stringent in the nation. Reproductive Health Services was a large abortion clinic in St. Louis. It had gone to court seeking to overturn the state's strict regulations.

The *Webster* case offered a fairly straightforward choice between two basic points of view. One view held that states had the right to regulate abortion. The other held that no one could deprive a woman of her right to kill her preborn child. The decision was a strong affirmation of the states' right to "regulate" abortion and thus a perceived victory for the pro-life cause. But to turn an old saying around, this particular silver lining had a large, black cloud attached.

In its opinion, the court said that state legislatures had the right to assert that human life begins at the point of fertilization if they *believed* that to be the case. This, in fact, was the basis on which the Missouri law was written. The court did not say whether such a position was right or wrong, merely that states could assert it if they chose. Thus the court adopted one of the wimpiest, trendiest positions imaginable—"it's true for you if you believe it"—and applied it to one of the most pressing questions imaginable—the definition of when human life begins. In effect, it made the personhood of the preborn child a matter of opinion—and of political horse-trading.

ALL applauded the *Webster* decision as a tiny step in the right direction, but not a very big step. It left unresolved the fundamental question of personhood. Worse, it clouded this vital matter in the minds of many people, including many pro-life people. The decision was, in retrospect, a disaster. But it did give us opportunities galore to educate people on the fact of personhood, which is not debatable.

I had the opportunity to appear on Oprah Winfrey's show with Molly Yard, the president of the National Organization for Women. Oprah was one of the most respectful television personalities I had ever met. She was pleasant off camera and discussed family with me, asked about my children and wondered aloud what brought me into this struggle. Never did I get the sense that she ever disagreed with my view. She was, to put it plainly, objective. Though I later learned that she supported "choice," it was not something she cared to make public on the show that day or privately in the "green room" where I was asked to wait until show time. Oprah's congeniality made my job a little easier. At least I would have one less opponent to debate.

Molly Yard, on the other hand, was a different story. Off camera she was the nicest lady anyone would ever want to meet. She went on and on about her grandchildren. But when those camera lights went on, she became a barracuda. She was out for blood. The funny thing was, though, that in her adamant dedication to abortion on demand, she forgot basic facts that my kids learned in Biology 101. She never used the word "mother" but preferred to relegate pregnancy to the category of an illness that needed a cure. In her mind abortion was similar to an antibiotic—it solved all problems simply. She was outraged that the state of Missouri would dare to make any attempt to regulate the practice of abortion, and told the audience that her organization, the National Organization for Women, would leave no stone unturned in making sure a woman's "right to abortion" was protected.

At one point, when I was discussing the personhood of the child, and the fact that abortion is an act of murder, I thought Molly was going to come unglued. She raised her voice and suggested that I was simply out of touch with reality. The audience guffawed, and roundly applauded Molly, but the scientific facts withstand even the most vociferous form of opposition. Even though we all know how shrill feminists can get, the fact is that my statements were made and heard. That is the beginning of teaching truth. No amount of catcalling is going to alter the facts.

Oprah, who listened attentively and became a referee of sorts, did give me the last word on two occasions, which meant, I think, that Oprah saw the logic in the pro-life argument. Even if she did not see it, she made sure the audience at least got the chance to think about it.

In 1989 I was face to face with Molly Yard, then president of NOW, on Oprah Winfrey's show.

~

In August, American Life League held an educational seminar in St. Louis to discuss the *Webster* decision and where to go next in the legislative arena. Brian Young, our staff attorney, had drafted 10 different legislative proposals that could be advanced in state legislatures. Each of the proposals was in line with the provisions of *Webster*, meaning that it should hold up in court. Each one was based on affirming the principle of personhood. Each one offered legislators an opportunity to cripple the abortion industry, to address the RU-486 problem, to provide new protection for the preborn child or to advance other concepts that did not violate personhood. More than 200 people attended the seminar. It was a great opportunity to discuss the issues, debate the proposals, and work toward a united position.

One group that did not attend—though it had been invited—was the National Right to Life Committee. Our efforts to include every group meant that we wrote letters of invitation, kindly answered by most groups, including those that could not be with us. However, NRLC never responded until days before the event. When their letter did arrive, it was a terse single sentence from Dr. John C. Willke, stating that they would be unable to attend.

As it turned out, NRLC had plans to host its own meeting. NRLC had drafted a legislative proposal it unveiled at a conference in Washington three months after ours. Their proposal was based on extensive polling data, which indicated that while the vast majority of Americans were opposed to abortion as a means of birth control, many thought abortion should be permitted in cases of rape, incest, fetal deformity, and serious threat to the health of the mother. NRLC had drafted a legislative proposal embodying these criteria and planned to launch it in all 50 state legislatures.

I was disappointed with the NRLC proposal for several reasons. The most obvious was that it failed utterly at the key point of the battle. By allowing for certain "exceptions," it undermined the principle of personhood, saying in effect that it was sometimes okay to kill babies. Spokesmen argued that "the people are with us," but that seemed unlikely. The public knew nothing of this legislative proposal prior its launch. The "abortion solely as a means of birth control" bill reminded me of a totally "pro-choice" approach since mothers could choose to kill their babies in certain cases.

I was saddened that NRLC had bypassed our August meeting and unveiled its proposal without inviting scrutiny from other groups and organizations. Once again, the pro-life movement was viewed as splintered with various organizations heading off in different directions. And this diagnosis of disarray once again failed to take note that unity can only be based on sound principle, not political pragmatism.

The media pounced on this latest pro-life political fracture, arguing accurately that the overall movement was weakened by public disagreements. Some in the press even pounced on NRLC's proposed exceptions to an outright ban on abortion, wondering how we could say that a human being begins at conception while providing reasons for killing those very human beings we claim to be defending. As liberal *Washington Post* columnist Richard Cohen wrote that year, "abortion opponents make the same argument [in favor of litmus tests for Supreme Court nominees], yelling murder and infanticide (but lowering their voices when it comes to rape or incest)."

For me, it was a sad turn of events. It provided many opportunities for me to comment on the problems that existed between American Life League and National Right to Life, but it was painful to discuss the basic reasons for this difficulty. I cannot tell you how often reporters would ask: "Isn't your purist approach actually hurting the movement's chances for success?" I would never hesitate to point out that any proposed legislation that allowed abortion to continue, even in a limited case like rape or incest, was legislation that condoned abortion and justified the practice. I would respond by defining abortion as an act that kills a person. But so many reporters refused to acknowledge this fact and continued to harp on their version of the truth.

While this was going on, I wondered: had some pro-life stalwarts simply given up on the principle of personhood? Were some of us really going to settle for protecting only some babies? Were politically motivated spokesmen who represented pro-life concerns going to be the ones to tell lawmakers which babies should be protected—and which babies it was okay to kill?

So many in our midst argue that compromise reflects the fundamental nature of politics. But when it comes to asking whether or not an innocent baby should be condemned to death in cases involving rape, incest, threat to the life of the mother or fetal deformity, I have to say that the clear answer should be "no." How could anyone claim that this is an acceptable strategy for a pro-life group, or politician?

I think a pro-life politician should never publicly support compromises that jeopardize even one life. We all know that a legislator often goes into a battle knowing, and aiming for, what he wants most. Then, along the way, he may see others water down his proposal, or otherwise weaken it. Then, when a final vote is required, he can choose to vote for it or against it or not to vote at all. But we who are the pro-life defenders in the battle, not the elected pro-life politicians, must never propose or in any way condone direct killing.

It is one thing when a politician compromises on financing a new highway. It is quite another when he compromises on something that will result in the execution of an innocent human being. Moreover, it is one thing when a politician compromises; it is quite another when lobbyists do the compromising for him. You can bet that lobbyists in other fields don't go to politicians and suggest ways in which their own interests can be undermined. Why, then, do so many pro-lifers?

When pro-lifers do this we make a mockery of our principles, and we undermine our own effectiveness as lobbyists. Politicians are already adept at compromising principles—they don't need us to do it for them. Unity comes about because of a total commitment to the truth. It will never be achieved as long as the fundamental principle of personhood is undermined.

~

One of the crowning achievements of 1989 for ALL was the production of "Champions for Life," a video starring six members of the 1987 Super Bowl Champion New York Giants. The video was made possible by the generosity of Wellington Mara, co-owner of the team. It was a tremendous success, something that could touch the hearts of young people in a new and exciting way. After all these years we finally had a tool to sway the teenager or college student who didn't want to buy the phony "pro-choice" arguments.

Paul and I traveled to Germany to give a set of seminars to the American pro-lifers connected to the hospital in Heidelberg. They wanted to do more for expectant mothers, and asked us to come and help them get organized. I recall the invitation to this very day, because it came from one our dearest fellow pro-lifers, Stephen Spaulding, M.D., who now practices medicine in New York.

As the year drew to a close, I found myself praying more and more that we would not let ourselves be swayed either by the disappointments of politics, by our own human frailty, or by the fleeting pleasures of momentary success. It is so easy to get caught up in the excitement of a television appearance, an appointment with a prominent government leader, or an ovation at a speech.

Whether in the face of failure or success, we need humility. In less time than we'd like to think, we will be gone and our deeds—even our names—forgotten. All that counts is whether we have faithfully done what our Lord has asked of us. He will never forget us.

~

Daddy had a major heart attack barely a week before Christmas. We had planned a traditional family Christmas at home—both Hugh and Cathy would be home from school—but those plans had to change. Because Christy was still suffering from her as-yet-undiagnosed illness, I decided to take her with me. Off we went to California.

The situation was worse than I had anticipated. Daddy's condition was quite serious, the doctors said. There was only one heart surgeon in the West who could perform the surgery he needed—and even then it was unclear if Daddy would be strong enough to survive. The rest of the family flew out to join us. Daddy went into surgery on Christmas Eve.

I went to Mass and spent most of the day in the chapel praying. Tears streamed down my face as I gave my stepfather over to the Lord. I tried to pray simply—God's will be done. I knew it wasn't right to try to tell God what to do. But, I must confess, much of my praying probably sounded like precisely that.

Daddy survived the emergency quadruple-bypass surgery. But he was hanging on by a thread. The doctor was not very encouraging. For days, Daddy lay in an intensive care unit, hooked up to what seemed like dozens of monitors, machines and feeding devices. If he did not show marked improvement soon, the doctor said, his chances of survival would become virtually nil.

Our prayers became increasingly urgent. Here lay a man, only 64 years old, who had given himself to our mother so unselfishly for so long, and who had poured himself out for us as well. The thought of losing him was more than my sisters and I could bear.

Almost miraculously, it seemed, his condition began to improve. Within a few days he was unhooked from most of the machines. By the time we returned home he was smiling, happy, and in full control of the situation. His biggest concern was whether or not he would be allowed to drive his car.

None of us had ever received a better Christmas present. All we could say was, "Thank you, Lord, for loving Daddy, and for allowing us to have him with us a little while longer."

Chapter Seventeen

Betrayal and Unity

1990

Justice will bring about peace; right will produce calm and security.
                              —Isaiah 32:17

Sometimes things happen where you least expect them. Who would have imagined that after years of conflict, debate and activity in places like Washington and New York, the pro-life controversy of the year would erupt in Idaho?

But that is exactly what happened. I suppose I shouldn't have been surprised. As I continued to attend daily Mass, I was overwhelmed by the truth of the lessons I was reading in *The Imitation of Christ*, a spiritual classic that I think is "must" reading for everyone who is trying to serve the Lord. The closer I grew to the Lord in prayer and in the Eucharist, the clearer it became that those who follow him would share in his trials and sufferings. What happened in Idaho definitely fit the mold.

The model legislation prepared by the National Right to Life Committee—the one that would restrict abortion while making exceptions in cases of rape, incest, and so on—had been passed in the Idaho legislature and now lay on the desk of Governor Cecil Andrus, awaiting his signature. Governor Andrus was thought to be pro-life. He had said previously that he would sign a bill limiting abortion as long as it contained the familiar array of "exceptions." Now, such a bill lay before him. It needed only a stroke of his pen to become the strictest anti-abortion law in the nation.

But in the end, he reneged. Rather than keep his word, he vetoed the very bill he had said would satisfy him. I can't say I

I visit Senator Jesse Helms to present him with a gift for him and his wife.

was completely surprised. Betrayal is in the very nature of compromises. As soon as we make exceptions to abortion, failure is assured.

I remember long discussions about this with our affiliate group in Idaho, with our staff and with elected officials in the state. The level of frustration was so high that I urged everyone involved to simply pray for God's will. We all found that by entrusting our concerns to Him, a peace came about that allowed us to persist. We knew that compromise could never be God's way of protecting His children. The failure of that Idaho governor to keep his word was a stunning example of the deception that is always the fruit of any effort that contradicts pro-life principle.

~

ALL's major event of the year was the pro-life show of shows, called "Unity 90." Our staff took great pride in the countless hours poured into planning. We hoped to receive satellite appearances or taped addresses from a number of world-renowned religious leaders. Because many of our staffers were Catholic, the two people topping the list were Pope John Paul II and Mother Teresa.

In writing to the Vatican, we knew that chances were very slim that the Holy Father would actually agree to a taped message, but we had to try. We did receive an amazing letter from his secretary of state. But when we began writing to Mother Teresa, there were no answers to our first three letters. As planning for our conference program book was nearing completion, it appeared that we were not going to receive a response. Someone said it might not be a bad idea to call Calcutta and find out if our letters had even arrived.

I got the phone number and made the call, after checking the time difference to be sure it was daytime in India. I said, "Hello. This is Judie Brown of American Life League in the United States, and I am calling to speak with Mother Teresa." The voice on the other end of the phone said to me, "This is Mother Teresa, Judie. How are you?"

I lost my breath, and almost passed out. I just could not believe that this world-famous, saintly nun was answering her own phone at the convent. As you can imagine, I did become slightly tongue-tied but finally got my question out. She was so kind and we received a lovely letter from her that we read at the event.

Unity 90 was a four-day conference in Chicago with representatives from virtually every major pro-life organization. During the meeting we broadcast a three-hour videoconference that was beamed to more than 250 satellite locations throughout the country and around the world. Millions of people saw Unity 90.

Judge Robert Bork—a man so cruelly abused by the Senate during his Supreme Court confirmation hearings—was there along with his wife Mary Ellen. So were Cardinal John O'Connor, Dr. Jerry Falwell, Dr. Bernard Nathanson, Dr. Mildred Jefferson and many others.

For three hours on the evening of June 30, Americans got the chance to see how respectable, how caring, and how dedicated the pro-life movement is. There were compelling guest appearances by Chicago Bears football coach Mike Ditka and rape victim Kay Zibolsky. Rev. Wilbur Lane, 88 years old and completely blind, received our "Hero of the Year" award.

When the dust settled and the mail began to pour in, we learned that Unity 90 had helped spur the formation of several new pro-life groups, including one for policemen called Officers for Life. The event had played a direct role in saving babies' lives and had re-invigorated many pro-lifers suffering discourage-

Unity 90 featured more than 60 speakers including (clockwise) Congressman Henry Hyde (R-Ill.); Cardinal John O'Connor; Csaba Vedlik, lobbyist, American Life Lobby; Mildred F. Jefferson, M.D., president, Right to Life Crusade.

ment. It had given witness to the reality of pro-lifers being committed first to God, and then to the rights of the innocent.

~

Unity 90 was a great success—and it nearly destroyed us. After it was over, we went into a financial tailspin. I kept telling people it was all part of God's plan—that He wouldn't have brought us this far down the road just to shove us over a cliff.

Indeed the trials and tribulations did work out to our ultimate benefit. For the first time in our history, a group of businessmen came forward and offered to form a "kitchen cabinet," a group of advisors who guided us out of our dilemma and helped us with our financial decisions.

A remarkable man named Bob Thomas, who had suffered from polio since his early 20s, spoke to me about the need to be totally professional in every aspect of our corporate effort at American Life League. He told me he was certain we could identify a few good people, with corporate backgrounds, who could help guide us along the way. Between his personal contacts and our own, we established a group of advisors that included Father Mike Scanlon, Jerome Urbik, Frank Larkin and Roderick O'Neill.

In their own right, each of them had succeeded by the world's standards because of incisive business acumen. There is no doubt that God put this team together for us at precisely the right moment in time.

If not for them, ALL would not have become a vibrant organization. The rest of us have been so busy fighting the fight that we have never really learned about budgets, strategic plans, cash-flow statements, endowment funds, capital campaigns and the other things that organizations need.

Their efforts guided us along the path that has expanded our credibility among those of financial means. Jerome Urbik ultimately recommended a man to us who brought precision, excellence and incredible public accountability to American Life League.

This man was our treasurer, Joseph Pavlik, CPA. He is a member of a well-known Chicago-based accounting firm, and his dedication to precision in accounting is only exceeded by his amazing commitment to the babies. I deeply appreciate his time, talent and expertise. His demand that we perform according to the letter of the accounting law, in every aspect of our operation, protected us from many attacks, including an IRS audit that we later learned had been carried out by the criminal division of the IRS. We survived, thanks to our desire to put in place every accounting practice Joe recommended.

It is the Joe Pavliks of this world that have made my job so very full to the brim with blessings.

~

It turned out that 1990 was a watershed year for me. The ongoing pro-life struggle to maintain principle over politics taught me the price of fortitude. Unity 90 taught me the value of principle. The "kitchen cabinet" taught me how little I really knew about how to run an organization. Athletes for Life, in its second year, taught me how blessed the pro-life movement is with heroic figures.

But more important than any of this, it was one of my children who reminded me that in Christ it is possible to accomplish all things if only we remember how miniscule we are in the grand plan of things, and how imperative it is at every turn to trust Him totally.

During this year we finally discovered the cause of our daughter Christy's pain. We had been to more than a dozen doctors over the course of nearly 18 months. Christy had become so weak that she couldn't even go to school; I was helping a tutor who was teaching her at home. Her doctor explained that she had an enlarged colon—about three times normal size—and said he wanted to perform surgery to pare it down to size. Christy was in the hospital for less than a week. Four weeks after the operation she celebrated her 16th birthday, and she has been fine ever since.

When I reflect on Christy's struggle, the one thing that stands out in my memory is her smile. It's angelic to me, but then mothers have a way of thinking those things about their own children.

Chapter Eighteen

Verbal Fog

1991–1992

The wise man is cautious and shuns evil; the fool is reckless and sure of himself. The quick-tempered man makes a fool of himself, but the prudent man is at peace.
—Proverbs 14:16–17

Balancing the corporate structure and solid fiscal growth of American Life League against the needs of the ever-changing culture became a great challenge for me during the ensuing two years. There seemed to be an ever-growing attitude in the pro-life movement that pro-lifers were, or at least should be, wedded to the Republican Party. This was a disaster.

Some in our movement scoffed at the idea of proposing pro-life legislation based on the personhood principle. It was argued that such proposals were not realistic and would make our so-called Republican friends in office very uncomfortable. Such allegedly pro-life politicians based their anti-abortion position on poll data. As a result, these men and women espoused a right to abortion in cases of rape, incest and life of the mother. In a climate like this, our friends said, we could not reasonably expect a personhood-based legislative proposal to pass.

Please let me be clear on this point. This ominous political reality did not deter American Life League from supporting only those legislative measures which did not allow for exceptions or other life-diminishing language. But it did mean that our efforts were undermined from within the pro-life movement. While ALL continued to oppose abortion because every abortion kills a fellow human being, many in our ranks increasingly looked at this heinous act as an "issue" to be used to elect less than totally pro-life politicians.

As individuals began considering the race for president, we found ourselves examining people on the basis of their ability to articulate defense for all innocent human beings. We never paid attention to their party loyalty. Once again, it seemed, American Life League had drawn a line in the sand and we stood apart from the rest. The claim that we were being divisive arose again. My response was that those who drove a wedge between the children and the political landscape were the divisive ones.

Each time I traveled to give a speech, participated in a debate, or appeared on a call-in radio talk show, the questions would come flying at me. Usually, they were from fellow pro-lifers. The exchange often went like this:

"Mrs. Brown, did it ever occur to you that your position on politicians who describe themselves as pro-life is totally unrealistic and harms our cause? Don't you realize that if we listened to zealots like you, the pro-aborts would be elected and we would consistently lose?"

I would respond, "Please take a moment and consider what it means to be pro-life. If we pro-lifers say that abortion in the case of rape, incest and life of the mother is acceptable to us, then we are saying that we will tolerate some abortions. How can we argue that abortion murders a fellow human being and say at the same time that some abortions are acceptable?"

"Mrs. Brown, get real! Everyone knows that there are only a few abortions done in cases of rape, incest and life of the mother. If we support the candidate who calls himself pro-life, we can stop 98 percent of all abortions."

To which I would reply, "The politician who holds a flawed position needs our help so that he can articulate a principled position that does not allow for any abortion. We are not, as pro-lifers, called to make exceptions, even if only one baby will die as a result of our actions. We are called to be faithful to the absolute truth that every innocent human being must be protected by law and by the culture. So let's not talk about percentages when it comes to abortion; let talk about what an abortion does to a human being and make sure politicians understand that if they want to call themselves pro-life, they cannot support killing babies for any reason."

∾

I think what happened between the dawn of the 1992 election season and the actual election was a tragedy. During the early days of that campaign, vulnerable human beings in the womb did have a champion—Republican contender Patrick J. Buchanan. Known for his eloquence, quick wit, and what some would describe as abrasiveness, Buchanan made a strong effort to oppose the party favorite, George Bush. Pat bowed out of the race early, and that was sad. But there was a message in Pat Buchanan's campaign that rang true. Here was a man who could run for office while at the same time being proud of his faith in God, and his commitment to all preborn children. He might have done poorly in the early days of that race, but he set a standard that would not be denied. He stood on principle and did not waver.

Buchanan did not do well because too many pro-lifers vowed to support the "popular" man rather than the principled man. In a primary race between Buchanan and Bush, they argued, Bush could win but Buchanan could not. Pro-lifers claimed that to beat the pro-abortion Democrat, they would have to support a "viable" candidate, and that would be Bush, not Buchanan. So they worked against Buchanan who, they said, was a loser.

Pat and I had become friends, and I wanted him to know that, at least in my opinion, he was the only Republican any pro-lifer, in good conscience, could support. He was kind in his description of those who opposed him and said that he knew, win or lose, that his position was right, and that was all that really mattered. This is why I have such high regard for Buchanan.

Ultimately, America faced a choice between George Bush, who gave lip service to saving the babies, and a little-known man from Arkansas, William Jefferson Clinton, who wowed the women, spoke in parables of confusion and ultimately won the White House by a plurality. Clinton, the nice guy from Arkansas, played well with an electorate that was fed up with Washington politicians and really looking for a change.

∽

On the legislative front, during those two years, nothing much happened that was noteworthy, but the Supreme Court dished out a decision in *Planned Parenthood v. Casey*. This decision effectively enshrined abortion and contraception into the Constitution. Here are a few examples of what the court had to say:

> "A state may not prohibit any woman from making the ultimate decision to terminate her pregnancy before viability"; and "the State ... may ... regulate, and even proscribe, abortion except where it is necessary, in appropriate medical judgment, for the preservation of the life or health of the mother."

In other words, the U.S. Supreme Court once again, by use of the word "health," in effect sanctioned abortion on demand throughout all nine months of pregnancy. There are many who believe that if a few members of the Supreme Court were replaced, then the court would overturn the *Roe v. Wade* and *Doe v. Bolton* decisions of 1973. But the court, in 1992, affirmed everything that a different court decided in 1973. In other words, the United States Supreme Court was not about to overturn *Roe* and *Doe*.

Let me share one more Casey statement with you. It is undoubtedly the most chilling phrase in the entire decision: "at the heart of liberty is the right to define one's concept of existence, of meaning, of the universe, of the mystery of life."

Can you believe it? The court recognized the illegitimate power a mother has to define for herself whether or not her child exists and, further, whether or not her child is meaningful. This one statement put the Supreme Court and the culture on a collision course with God and His authority over creation.

~

American Life League began producing a five-minute radio program designed to help people think about what they could do to work against the evil of abortion. We had thousands of people listening to it all across America. It was so much fun to make these daily recordings that it hardly seemed right. While it is true that we were battling an act that kills babies, it was enjoyable to be creating a program that countered the death peddlers.

At the same time we laid the groundwork for producing a weekly half-hour television program. We called it "Celebrate Life TV."

Sports Illustrated recognized Athletes for Life with a review of the *Champions for Life* video. The magazine panned the program as tasteless. Now, you could say that this is really not encouraging, but what this meant to me was that for the first time, a mainstream sports magazine was recognizing the fact that there are professional athletes who believe in the sanctity of human life. The guy who wrote the article was wrong about the video, but he watched it. Praise God!

In 1992, American Life League launched *African American Committee News*. The African-American Committee, led by Rev. Ronald O. Ross, set a standard for the pro-life movement, focusing on the need to reach out to minority families through spokesmen who could effectively change the way abortion was viewed. Remembering the early success of Rev. Hiram Crawford in Illinois, and the speaking abilities of Rev. Ross, we could help others form such groups in their communities, too.

Less than 13 percent of the American population is black, and yet nearly 30 percent of all abortions are done on black mothers. Now, to my mind, that is discrimination of the worst possible kind.

Christy talked to me about teens and how we could get more young people involved in pro-life activism. She said she would be willing to write a column for our magazine, and she would be interested in helping launch new activities for teens at American Life League. I know it is her vivacious personality that made the difference, and so it is not surprising that Teen American Life League attracted young commentators, debaters and activists from across the nation. At 16 years of age, Christy combined enthusiasm, the gift of gab and a penchant for poetry that made her so popular with her peers that people couldn't wait to read her monthly columns. She got so much mail that we thought of getting her a secretary.

During this year I was involved in intense discussions with people in Congress and with Secretary of Health and Human Services Louis Sullivan. ALL opposed any use of fetal tissue from children who had been intentionally aborted. Congress did not appear to have a problem with such tissue harvesting. The House voted to lift the long-standing ban on federal funding of fetal tissue experimentation. The reason seemed to be that it was better to use the body parts from babies killed by abortion than to let them go to waste. Now, no politician actually said it exactly that way, but I hope you get the point. Members of Congress favored this disgusting practice and made no bones about it.

At the time, I told the media, "This bill does nothing more than allow abortionists to be paid for delivering a dead baby and then be paid again for delivering the tissue of that dead baby to researchers."

I had many opportunities to observe exactly how confusing this subject was, even for many pro-lifers. It was an eye-opener for me, one that I even discussed with Hugh, Cathy and Christy.

I wanted a fresh perspective from them to make sure that my thinking was not confusing to those who would listen to what American Life League had to say.

I guess my biggest surprise in having these talks with my own children was their personal dismay that anyone would consider using any part of a baby killed by abortion, regardless of the "humanitarian" reason given. I told them the problem we faced was one of denial and they agreed. It was clear to all of us, at least, that even Secretary Sullivan, who wanted people to think he was pro-life, viewed the body of a dead baby as a field ready for harvest.

After my discussions with my children, I decided that the tactics we used to expose this atrocity had better be clear, succinct and graphic. Otherwise, people would believe the televised arguments that the tissues from aborted fetuses (they never used the word "baby") could allegedly provide treatment and even healing for victims of Parkinson's, Alzheimer's and AIDS. The media never gave concrete examples to prove such statements; they just made the statements.

This struggle to expose the ghastly fetal tissue research practice convinced us, more than ever, that personhood was the only goal worthy of our pursuit. If the preborn child could be legally recognized as a person under the Constitution, no more arguments about how to use his dead body would ever again be held. At least, that was our hope.

American Life League issued the "Personhood Manifesto," which presented a clear statement designed to help leaders and grassroots Americans envision the person at fertilization when he or she is smaller than the head of a pin. We were convinced that for every rotten thing that goes on in our world there was a positive, joyful antidote. In 1992, the manifesto filled that bill. It gave us the "piece of paper" we needed to set before the Secretary Sullivans and Senator John McCains of the world, men not so much dedicated to abortion as confused about what abortion does to real, living people.

∼

On the home front, things were really getting interesting. Christy had overcome her illness, graduated from high school and chose photography as her field of interest. Christy's growing interest in photography, developing her own film and strange photo shoots in the middle of the night introduced us to many new phrases and techniques we had never heard of before and still don't fully appreciate. But she excelled in her field from her first class at the local community college.

Hugh completed his college education and proposed to his girlfriend Ann in 1991. They set their wedding date on November 21, 1992.

Ann's parents planned the wedding with the greatest detail. Even though my dear father could not fly on airplanes because of his weakened heart, he wanted desperately to be at the wedding. So he traveled by train from California to Virginia.

Paul had a surprise up his sleeve for our 25th wedding anniversary, December 30, 1992. We had a lovely Mass to renew our vows and a black-tie dinner-dance to celebrate the occasion.

So, while the pro-life movement was sinking to a new low in some ways, our family was growing spiritually, emotionally and in sheer numbers.

Daddy at Hugh and Ann's wedding, 1992, his last visit.

Chapter Nineteen

Good-bye, Daddy

~

1993

In him who is the source of my strength, I have strength for everything.
                                    —Philippians 4:13

The year got off to a very exciting start for us. Paul and I spent our anniversary traveling to Brazil. It was so remarkable to see a part of the world we had only read about.

~

In June my father became very ill. Paul and I flew out to Los Angeles to be with him. He had been taken to the emergency room of a local hospital and, unable to speak, he had written on a pad of paper that he wished to have a tracheotomy tube placed in his lungs to help him breathe. No one in that emergency room was paying any attention to his requests at all. In fact one nurse said to me: "Hey, I can't understand what he wants." We gave Daddy a clipboard and a pen, on which he wrote a note I could completely understand. It said, simply, "I want the tube."

This incredible experience made me wonder how many patients like him, who have no loved ones standing by, die because no one is paying attention to them. Or worse, how many "caretakers" have consciously decided that a person is about to die anyway, so why bother? We read about such cases all the time. But when it is your own father, and you see the apathy right there looking at you, it really is scary.

Daddy recovered and went home from the hospital to live with his sister, Mildred. But in late July we got another call. He was seriously ill again, so I flew out to be with him. Again, no one expected him to leave the hospital, but he fooled everyone and came home on a Friday. I left that Sunday to go back home, convinced that he would be all right. I assured my aunt that she should go ahead and leave town, as she had planned a trip for later that week. Fortunately, she did not listen to me.

I was home one day, and the call came that he had been taken to the hospital again and was in intensive care. I flew out with Christy, who had been preparing to leave for New York to start school in a few weeks. But she wanted to be with her favorite person, her grandfather. On August 10 he died. Daddy's heart had simply given up after so many battles fought so valiantly. He never got out of intensive care, but he knew we were there with him. Daddy died in peace and without pain.

I have often compared him to the Good Samaritan. Daddy had no time for gossip, no time for complaining, and no time for people who had a negative view of the world. He lived with rose-colored glasses every minute of his life, regardless of the circumstances.

Hugh could not be at the funeral but he wrote a great tribute to his grandfather. I will miss my dad just as much as I miss my mother, but even though they are not here in a physical sense, I sometimes feel they are still taking good care of me.

~

At the beginning of 1993, American Life League launched a test newsletter for our supporters and friends. It was called "Prayer and Fasting to End Abortion." We sent this out quarterly, and for a couple of years it was well received, or so I thought. But it became clear that too many of us believed that sacrifice was not necessary to end the senseless slaughter of innocent persons. It is clear to me now that we expected too much from people who barely ever heard the word "abortion" during a Sunday sermon, let alone a preacher who extolled the value of penitential fasting.

It was time to take a hard look at those pulpits. It occurred to me that this meant including the clergy in our efforts in a meaningful, extensive way.

American Life League was once again in the eye of a storm, and it was a gentle man who placed us there—Cardinal John O'Connor. He called me to talk about a new program called Priests for Life. Its purpose was to help priests use the pulpit in defense of the dignity of the human person. Cardinal O'Connor asked me if ALL would help Father Frank Pavone expand the organization. We agreed to be part of the start-up effort in New York, with the understanding that, as Priests for Life gained stability, we would cease our funding. I looked forward to homily outlines, teaching tools and other specifics that Cardinal O'Connor said Priests for Life would produce for priests around the nation.

Of all the prelates in the Church in America during the 1980s and 1990s, Cardinal O'Connor was the one who always had a kind word to say about American Life League. He never failed to make his defense of the innocent his number one priority.

∾

The Personhood Manifesto continued to gain credibility within the pro-family movement. At the same time, ALL took up the challenge of establishing an affiliate program to assist local grassroots groups in defending the vulnerable.

We continued to air "Celebrate Life TV," including a six-month stint of back-to-back programs on National Empowerment Television. "Celebrate Life TV" was far ahead of its time. Had we known then what we know now about things like viewer counts and friendly television networks such as EWTN, things might have gone better. But as it turned out, 1993 was the final production year for this project. The costs became higher than we could bear.

∾

Also in 1993, I received another surprise from Mother Teresa. We sent her a galley proof copy of my book, and asked her if she might write a word or two about it for us. Not only did she write an incredible endorsement, which we have on the back cover, but also she sent me a special prayer she asked me to say for an end to abortion in the world.

After that I heard from her on several occasions, and in 1994 received a Miraculous Medal from her. Her friendship, because it was based on our mutual concern for God's little ones, made

With Cardinal John O'Connor at the March for Life.

me more convinced than anything else that those who are true servants of God are the most humble people. Mother Teresa never lost sight of whom she was representing on earth, and she always reflected His joy.

∾

Remember RICO? A related threat, FACE, came along in 1993. This time we decided not to take this anti-free-speech law sitting down. The FACE Act (Freedom of Access to Clinic Entrances) was designed with only one thing in mind: to discriminate against pro-lifers who peacefully protest. The bill smacked of billion-dollar access to the halls of power by the fat cats of the abortion industry. ALL, always dedicated to making an effort at being the giant killer, sued the federal government.

My grandma used to say: "Give it all you've got, Judie, but never forget that God will take care of it. Still, you've got to try."

We gave it our best shot. We sued, but we lost. It became painfully clear in 1993 that the government was willing to take whatever steps it could to chill, if not eradicate, any visible protest against surgical abortion. FACE is still used as a weapon against those who defend the innocent.

On the political front, a bad situation was getting progressively worse. During 1993 America witnessed a first: pro-life endorsement of political candidates such as Kay Bailey Hutchison, who won a U.S. Senate seat in Texas. She was considered pro-life only because she opposed the Freedom of Choice Act, a pro-abortion bill that never had a chance of passing. Support for Hutchison translated into a new definition of pro-life in politics. It meant that a person could gain the pro-life label while doing absolutely nothing to advance total protection for the innocent.

Conservative columnist Cal Thomas wrote of Hutchison's race: "The key to this race lies in what the social conservatives decide to do. Many pro-life, pro-family voters supported Republican Rep. Jack Fields of Houston and Joe Barton of Ennis. They can now refuse to vote for Mrs. Hutchison because she is 'pro-choice' on abortion (but moderately so—she favors parental consent laws and restrictions on abortion after viability, except in the rare instance when the life of the mother is threatened), or they can engage in principled pragmatism and vote for Mrs. Hutchison."

It is sad, but true, that frequently "winning" at any cost becomes the goal, and for those of us who are called to this battle, that must never be our point of view. "Winning" should only mean protecting the vulnerable and doing all we can possibly do to save every life, not just the politically correct lives. So when I say something like "being moderately pro-life is like being moderately pregnant," people get angry with me.

I really do not know what a "social conservative" is, but I do know that the child whose life hangs in the balance each time a mother is contemplating an abortion is not a conservative or a liberal. No, that baby is someone who may never get to choose anything in life if her mother chooses abortion. So I really do not care what a voting block does, but I do care about what a person will do when casting a vote. I do not believe that there is any such thing as "principled pragmatism." I cannot tolerate a little abortion any more than you can tolerate a little murder in your family. A crime is a crime, period.

～

As if the Hutchison race wasn't bad enough, Congress watered down the Hyde Amendment to include exceptions for rape and incest. When first introduced in 1976, the Hyde Amendment was designed to prohibit any spending of taxpayer dollars on abortion.

I got into a heated exchange with Congressman Hyde. I simply could not understand why he would allow his name to be attached to an amendment that permitted payment for abortion when the whole idea behind the original Hyde Amendment was to ban tax dollars from being used to pay for abortion. He told me privately that he would not permit it; but in public he did the opposite. I could not let it go, so I sent him a telegram and issued a news release condemning this action. The interviews began, and the congressman wanted nothing further to do with me. I had failed to play the game according to pro-life political rules.

As a result of this sham, American Life League called on pro-life leaders to come together in a quiet, off-the-record gathering, to renew our dedication to principle, and to agree to never again support compromise. Sadly the meeting did not take place. Our invitation was rejected, without comment, by all national right-to-life groups involved in political action. We were dismissed as nothing but idealistic purists with no understanding of political reality. Now, compromise was "in," and that meant American Life League was "out."

~

During the final weeks of 1993 ALL unveiled its pro-life response to the living will. Our document, called the Loving Will, had been under development for three years. This project would provide those with concerns about their end-of-life care with peace of mind in knowing that no one would intentionally kill them. We introduced the Loving Will as groups rallied in state capitals across the land to promote "physician-assisted suicide," a catchphrase for murder.

In fact, my mother could have been the victim of those very people. She was, to those who support the Culture of Death, a person who was expendable. In the eyes of those who promote killing the infirm, the elderly and the dying, she could offer nothing to society and therefore she would have been easily relegated to the status of non-person. The people who promote death place emphasis on how "useful" you are, rather than the inherent dignity you possess as a human being created in the image and likeness of God. They call themselves compassionate people who believe everyone should have a *right to die.*

I loved my Mom more than words can say and cherished every moment I had with her. She was, even in her weakened state, a beacon of wisdom. So how could I fail to do everything in my power to make sure that everyone's loved ones, regardless of their condition, were protected?

~

Christmas is a time of exceeding joy, and that year, recalling my Daddy's passing and the pro-life struggle to protect those who were deemed to be "unwanted," there was a scripture passage that rang in my ears, and still resonates in my heart:

> *For I am certain of this: neither death nor life, no angel, no prince, nothing that exists, nothing still to come, not any power, or height or depth, nor any created thing, can ever come between us and the love of God made visible in Christ Jesus Our Lord.*
>
> —Romans 8:38-39

Chapter Twenty

Religious Right?

1994

The Lord indeed, knows how to rescue devout men from trial.

—2 Peter 2:9

When William Jefferson Clinton took office in 1993, he promised to rid the country of as many preborn children as possible. Well, he never said that—not in so many words. But his actions spoke louder than words.

On January 22, the anniversary of the *Roe v. Wade* and *Doe v. Bolton* decisions, Clinton, by executive order, lifted the ban on human embryo research, struck down the Reagan language that prohibited the U.S. from being involved in foreign aid programs involving abortion, eradicated the abortion-counseling prohibition (so-called "gag" rule) from federally funded programs, and swiftly sent the Justice Department scurrying after ways to put as many pro-lifers as possible in jail. There was absolutely no doubt about the president's agenda, and pro-life America was in a spin.

⁓

While all of us were attempting to recover from the blows dealt by the president, Hillary Clinton was also carefully examining ways to translate the Culture of Death basics into a new health care policy. There was talk of rationing health care based on the age and health of the patient. There was talk of making abortion a primary health care "need" for women.

When it became clear that Hillary's health care plan was actually going to move from the secret meetings in New York City to the desks of congressmen in Washington, we got busy in a hurry. As soon as the plan was published, we were hard at work deciphering it, word by evil word. We published a handbook for grassroots pro-lifers that detailed the many anti-life facets of this thousand-page proposal, and we constantly warned pro-lifers about the threats to life and liberty cleverly buried in the language of the plan.

The overall message was that government would replace parents by doling out "health care services" to unsuspecting children. I remember one mother who called our office in a frenzy because she was concerned that schools would be authorized to give her child all manner of "help" including birth control without her ever knowing about it. Looking back now, it is a blessing that the Clinton health care plan of 1993 failed, though much of what Hillary wanted has been enacted in various state and federal plans.

～

Attorney General Janet Reno, who made sweeping derogatory statements against pro-life activists, was having a field day sending federal marshals to abortion mills. Their assignment was to protect those who slaughter the babies, no matter what needed to be done. Is it any wonder that pro-life direct action nearly ceased to exist? Few pro-lifers felt energized to test the law, particularly when they reflected on the attorney general who would enforce it.

At a Catholic parish in Connecticut, the pro-life coordinator had been working with others in her parish to organize a Rosary vigil outside the local abortion mill. Just as she found four or five of her fellow parishioners to participate in the vigil, a man from the parish came to their meeting and told them if they prayed outside that mill, they would all go to jail and maybe even lose their homes. You can imagine what happened. No one wanted to participate.

This poor woman called me in tears. She had worked so hard and could not believe that praying would land a person in jail. Over a period of two weeks, with a lot of gentle urging, she agreed to do a few things that would assure success. I asked her to meet with the chief of police and find out what she needed to do to use the sidewalk for prayer. She did that and the police department was most cooperative and grateful to her for coming to them. But most encouraging was the fact that the police chief assured her that no one in his jurisdiction was going to be jailed for praying.

Finally, the Rosary vigil occurred, with 10 people praying and singing that first Saturday. What is great about this story is that years later that vigil continues, the numbers have grown, and not one person has ever been arrested for praying.

The jury is still out on the draconian RICO and FACE laws. There are so many challenges continuing to come through the court system that we may yet see RICO and FACE overturned. But that time would be much sooner than later if all groups united in efforts to test the constitutionality of such laws.

However, we must not succumb to the fear that might prevent us from public witness. We must continue to participate in public demonstrations and prayer vigils against abortion and euthanasia. At the same time pro-lifers have to pursue ways to challenge the laws in court until integrity returns to judicial decision-making.

~

In another form of activism, the kind I love to talk about, Michigan state senator Jack Welborn had introduced a "memorial tribute to the souls of the dead babies taken from us." This small piece of paper sent chills down my spine the first time I read it. Having had three wonderful children myself, the words brought tears to my eyes. Here are a few lines from his tribute:

> *You are gone from us now after a very brief time in the realm of human existence, but you will never be forgotten by those of us who tried to save your life. We will never forget that you suffered the most brutal death imaginable—poisoned, burned, ripped, and violently vacuumed from your mothers' wombs. You died innocent and defenseless in a place designed by God to nurture you and keep you safe, a place whose sanctity was defiled by depraved grown-ups who turned it into a horror chamber of death ... We apologize for the society that turned its back on you and let you die. ... Those of us who have been fighting to stop the killing of babies like yourselves will channel our grief for you into the fight to guarantee the right to life—We will make sure that you did not die in vain.*

Praying the rosary with pro-lifers in Scotland.

Such expressions of sincere sorrow for the loss of individual human beings remind me that we must never give up.

~

As 1994 Congressional races began heating up, the thing that really began to bother me was the devaluation of principle in the pro-life ranks.

I believe that if Jesus were instructing His disciples today in political strategy and in protecting the weak and the vulnerable, He would expect His disciples to teach and preach the commandments and the beatitudes. What better political strategy could anyone want, after all?

Some might think my proposal is seriously flawed because it doesn't take into consideration modern political realities, but I would suggest that this is precisely why we should embrace the strategy. How do you promote conversion if you have no sound platform on which to stand and teach?

As Senator Jesse Helms once told me, "Judie, those of us who are in politics love to see our name on the ballot, and we love to be the winner. So my advice to you is this—never put your faith in any man, but keep it with God and hold us accountable, even when we tell you that you should know your place and keep quiet."

Senator Helms' statement is true, and I have taken his advice to heart.

~

To be labeled pro-life in the 1994 Congressional races meant that you could oppose one particular type of abortion, or at the most, government spending on abortion.

Calling yourself pro-life also meant that you could support abortion reform that included exceptions for rape, incest, and the life of the mother because the public supported such a position. If you happened to measure up to these drastically reduced standards, you could expect endorsements from the National Right to Life Committee, Christian Coalition activists and many so called "right-wing" or "religious right" groups.

To the average political candidate in 1994, being pro-life meant doing as little as you could for preborn children. It meant that nearly anyone who opposed just one percent of all abortions could wear the pro-life label and get positive attention from Christian and conservative groups. It meant that the American people who really trusted pro-life leaders to tell them who was and who wasn't pro-life were being misled and deceived. This is hypocrisy of the worst kind, formulated on half-truths described politely as political incrementalism.

I challenged this mindset at every turn. I attended meetings with fellow pro-lifers during which I scolded them for not having the integrity to stand up and proclaim the full truth and demand that politicians do likewise. I did not do this with disrespect or a flair for the dramatic. I usually asked a lot of questions, as I did in an exchange with a fellow from the Christian Coalition.

"Frankly," I said, "I do not understand how you can in good conscience give a pro-life seal of approval to a man who favors abortion in cases of rape, incest, and life of the mother and says that he is only opposed to federal funding of abortion."

My friend replied, "Judie, you just aren't very politically astute. We have to face the reality that if we do not support this guy, and get our people out in the trenches working for his election, then the opponent will win and we will be faced with a Democrat who favors abortion on demand."

"What you seem to be telling me is that the mere fact that your guy is a Republican is better than if he were a Democrat, regardless of what his position is on abortion," I responded.

"Yep, that's it, Judie," he said. "We know that the Republican Party is the pro-life party, and this guy will help us retain a pro-life, Republican majority in the House."

"But," I noted, "if a tough vote comes up in the House, and the pro-lifers are asked to cast a vote on a bill that does not coincide with this man's position, he is going to vote pro-abortion. Right?"

"Yep, that's right, Judie. So, we will make sure that only bills that are appealing to our friends ever get introduced or come up for a vote. By doing that, we are protecting our friends."

I looked this political strategist in the face, and said with as much calm as I could muster, "This is the most incredible conversation I have ever had. What you are telling me is that you intend to work against the possible introduction of a bill that might actually stop all abortions. What you are really saying is that you want to make sure that this man is comfortable with the laws that are introduced, even if that means no babies will be saved while he is in office."

"Judie, I am sorry that you do not agree with my tactical plan, but I am the expert," he said. "You go ahead and keep doing the wonderful job you do educating people on principle, but leave the politics to me."

I felt like weeping at that moment, but I said a silent prayer of thanks that God had given me the ability to stay the course. The battle American Life League was waging was obviously not the same battle many of our friends were involved in. It was nice to hear it, frankly and honestly, from a man who had the guts to tell me precisely what I had suspected for so long.

~

When the pro-life movement started, our goal was to protect all preborn children by passing a constitutional amendment. We knew back in the early 1970s that every single abortion killed one of our brothers or our sisters, and we refused to tolerate this immoral act. But by the mid-90s that vision had been altered by moral relativism—a necessary commodity in the political game —meaning that a little bit of abortion is OK if it serves the political agenda of the pro-life political experts.

The eight-second sound bite designed to appease our political friends became more relevant than the words of truth. I would love to hear someone from the National Right to Life Committee or the Christian Coalition come out and publicly say, "Party politics is not what we are about. We want candidates to run for public office who will battle to protect every innocent person from conception/fertilization without exception and without apology."

But the sad fact is that we live in a society that teaches tolerance for all. Somewhere along the way the "religious right" had taken a wrong turn. God had become a subject not discussed in certain circles. He had been relegated to Sundays only, and never during political gatherings.

We were told with great fanfare that the American people had elected the most pro-life Congress in the history of the movement. But I remember the new Speaker of the House, Newt Gingrich, being asked about legislation that would stop abortion. He said, simply, "Oh, we will get to that issue, but I am not certain what we will do about it right now."

History has now recorded that the infamous "Contract with America" had no room for the protection of our most vulnerable Americans—preborn children.

～

Along with the other challenges facing our movement at the time, we faced new concerns over the revelation that many childhood vaccines were manufactured using cells from intentionally aborted babies. This came to a head in 1994 when a Catholic prep school in England refused to participate in the government program to vaccinate children against measles and rubella. The rubella component of the vaccine, according to reports, was originally derived from aborted babies. I heard about this from a frantic mother in Ohio who called to tell me that she had read the story and wondered whether to have her children vaccinated. I was shocked. Here we were in our own family with two little grandchildren, and the story was out that some childhood vaccines were tainted because tissue and cells from aborted children had been used.

I called on our friends at Pharmacists for Life International for advice on what to do. Fortunately, they were way ahead of us and were already studying the situation carefully.

As if this wasn't bad enough, the Food and Drug Administration was toying with the idea of approving abortive chemicals such as the morning after pill, RU-486, and other products designed to kill babies.

In addition, the National Institutes of Health convened a panel to discuss human embryo research. The NIH panel concluded that using embryonic humans for research purposes was not only ethical but a must.

Bill Clinton's dreams were all coming true. There were going to be more babies killed than ever before.

What reasons could the scientific community possibly give for directly killing embryonic babies for research purposes? Enlarging scientific knowledge in areas of reproductive health was one argument. They were saying, "If we use embryonic people for experimentation, by using their body parts for research, we can develop new and better ways to make people sterile so that they don't have to have babies at all." The scientists didn't explain it quite that way, of course.

The media reported that the panel would only be using embryos younger than 14 days of age. The reporters did not state that these embryos were actually human beings, but rather "cell mass." Never mind that the federal government had banned taxpayer funding of the procedures in question; the panel wanted to change the law. In fact, the panel fashioned a lobbying effort designed to intimidate the Congress into falling over itself to help pay for the research that would result in millions of embryonic babies dying.

Now, think about this for a moment, please. I certainly thought about it, because of my young grandchildren. My grandchildren were never less human because they were smaller than the head of a pin. They did not magically become human beings because a panel decided it was time to call them that.

It would have been better for the American public if grandparents and parents had been appointed to that panel instead of the group Clinton nominated. Nobody on that panel discussed the value of the child—only the scientific benefits of research using the "cell mass." There was total denial when they were confronted with the scientific fact that a human being begins at fertilization. When I testified during their public hearings, I asked them to explain to me when a human being begins. The best response I got was, "We have no consensus."

~

Paul has often said that if anyone had told us how much fun it would be to be grandparents, we would have had the grandchildren first. Let me tell you, my personal life was filled with the joys of being a grandma—what a wonderful experience. I had always thought that motherhood was fantastic, but this was beyond compare. Where else can you divest yourself of all decorum to roll around on a floor, sound like an animal, and act like a complete and total nut? As a mom I had always been so worried about other aspects of raising our children that I rarely had the opportunity to make a total fool of myself. But all that changed when the grandkids came to visit.

Chapter Twenty-one

Celebrating the
Gospel of Life

~

1995

All scripture is inspired of God and is use-
ful for teaching—for reproof, correction,
and training in holiness so that the man of
God may be fully competent and equipped
for every good work.
—*2 Timothy 3:16–17*

On March 25, 1995, Pope John Paul II issued the extraordinary encyclical *The Gospel of Life (Evangelium Vitae)*. This 180-page document has been described as a "love letter" to all people of good will. Though it appeared cumbersome, I decided to read the entire thing. In the encyclical, we find the positive signs in our culture for hope and renewal and, most importantly, the inspiration to live the *Gospel of Life* every day.

We know that God calls us to a task He has specifically assigned to us. That's how God is. But sometimes that task seems so trivial in the context of world problems that we become convinced that our little piece of God's great plan is not all that important. This is why each of us needs to be affirmed and uplifted in our daily lives. We look at the ordinary things that we do every day and really can't see how they mesh with the big picture—saving souls and bringing our fellow human beings into a conversation with God. But the truth is that the simplest act of kindness can bring about amazing changes in the entire world.

Christ walked the earth and touched the lives of average people one by one. He brought the Good News to them by preaching, loving and healing. He was there, in the living room, in the town square, at the market. Every time we do something out of love and charity for someone else, even if that someone else does not notice what we have done, we are living the Gospel of Life.

Often, during the course of a day, interruptions occur that require my time and attention. Sometimes it is my grandson who needs a few hours of my time, or a friend who calls and seems to have so much to say that a phone call lasts forever. But when I turn from what I want to do to those things God is asking of me, I am living the Gospel of Life.

By being servants of life we are affirming God's love in our actions and our words. This is important because every pro-life good deed is a part of the plan our Father has for all mankind. We don't need to know that plan. But we do need to know that our daily effort contributes to it in ways we cannot even begin to comprehend.

The Gospel of Life teaches each of us is that in our daily lives there are countless opportunities to thank God for loving us and breathing life into us by treating others in a way that is pleasing to Him.

∾

At American Life League we took the encyclical to heart. We decided to create a series of study guides—guides for a Bible study group, for a classroom discussion, and for the person who wished to study *The Gospel of Life* on his own. These books would help others grasp the inspiring words of this document and apply those words to their own lives.

I can look back on my pro-life journey and praise God that there is total affirmation in *The Gospel of Life* for the many controversial positions ALL has taken over the years. Pope John Paul II reminds us that every innocent human being is an expression of God's love for the world. He says that man is a reflection of God's love. How inspiring it is to sit back and think about that— to know that God created each one of us because He loves us and has shared His very being with us.

Imagine how exciting it was to attend a special meeting in the Vatican on *The Gospel of Life*! I gave a draft copy of our study guides to the Holy Father, who smiled and encouraged me while I stood there dumbfounded with tears in my eyes. It was an experience that is really difficult for me to describe.

∾

Congressman Bob Dornan's *Right to Life Act* was introduced and heralded by many pro-life leaders as a principled proposal that would literally put America's elected officials on record acknowledging personhood from conception. The sense of optimism and excitement over this bill was contagious. Personhood was back on the front burner, and we were thrilled.

∾

American Life League's powerful "face it—abortion kills" campaign went into high gear. People have told me it is one of the most potent sign campaigns in the history of the pro-life movement. It set the standard for many signs, T-shirts, sweatshirts, bumper stickers and other materials subsequently used to get the simple message across that abortion is an act that takes the life of a person. The power of that sign is the black-and-white format. The sign shows up in countless news photos and it is always easy to pick out and easy to read. Today thousands of these signs are carried across the nation.

~

During 1995 we worked with a coalition of groups to oppose the nomination of Henry Foster as surgeon general. A known abortion proponent with strange ideas about sex instruction for children, he was a mirror image of another infamous figure of the Clinton era: Joycelyn Elders. We got flack for doing this because some of our friends felt it was inappropriate to spend precious time and money opposing a nominee for surgeon general.

When I think of surgeons general, I think of doctors who still believe in the Hippocratic Oath and would never harm an innocent or vulnerable person. Henry Foster did not quite fit that description. We had to oppose him.

Just as our campaign was dying down, Congress introduced a welfare reform bill that could have forced many mothers toward abortion out of a sense of hopelessness. We had to

Paul and I with a presention for the Holy Father.

oppose the bill, and were joined in the effort by Congressmen
Chris Smith and Dale Kildee among others. Thank God, it failed.
But I got a few tongue-lashings over it. Even one of our board
members said to me, "Judie, you are wrong to pursue this line of
thinking. Welfare is bad for America and must be curtailed."

Though I agreed that welfare had gotten out of control, I
believed the mothers of preborn children should not be punished.

∽

College campuses are breeding grounds, in most cases, for
hatred of babies, disdain for Christianity and disrespect for the
sacramental union of marriage. On almost any campus these
days you can find a major or a minor in "women's studies" but I
dare you to identify a major or a minor on human life studies.
On far too many campuses, the Lord is relegated to a historic
footnote of old-fashioned "beliefs" no longer needed, and frequently replaced by a wide variety of pseudo-religious studies.
ALL's board responded by forming a campus outreach program.

My own observations underscored the value of that decision.
When Hugh was at the University of Maryland, the campus pro-
life group invited me to speak about abortion. I told the young
lady that if I accepted, I would provide the full picture, including facts on birth control, sexuality within marriage, and so on.
Because Hugh was there, I asked him if he could make it to the
speech. Paul was coming, too, and I thought it might be nice to
have us all together. Hugh agreed to be there, and promised that
he and a few of his friends would escort me on campus. Since
he played football, as did his friends, I felt as secure as the president feels with the Secret Service.

After the speech, the harrowing questions, antics and weird
behavior from the audience erupted. I met, face to face, with college students who were convinced that God was dead, who
knew that sexual relations should be practiced frequently and
with as many "partners" as possible, and who were vehement
about abortion as the "choice" of their generation. Try as I might,
logic was out the window with these people. I felt so sorry for
the pro-life group that had invited me, but as I later said to Hugh
and his pals, "This is a tragic statement on the level of ignorance

among the men and women receiving higher education. Their minds are in the gutter." Hugh responded without a blink, "Yeah, Ma. That's why I am so glad I had parents like you and Dad. This stuff is all over the place here."

While she was attending George Mason University, Cathy helped to organize pro-life efforts. Again, I went to give a talk, and though the audience was a bit less frenetic at George Mason, the tenor of the questions and comments was the same. I met and spoke privately with young men and women who had no idea what it meant to be chaste until marriage. They were convinced that marriage was "old hat" and determined to do whatever their basic instincts told them was a good idea. Conscience seemed to have left the building. I have always admired Cathy for her stalwart defense of life, but that experience showed me what a real challenge it is for our youth to get out on the front lines and defend life.

During her time at New York University, Christy got into more spats with people in the Tisch School of Art than I ever knew about. She would often tell me how interesting she found it to tell a class, during a discussion about some topic or other, that she was a virgin. How this came up during photography classes on history and art, I am not sure, but it did. The most amazing aspect of it was her stories about the kids who would come up to her later, privately in the hall or on the street, and say that they were virgins, too, but that they would never say so in public.

As pro-lifers, each of us needs to understand that if we are to succeed, we must first and foremost raise our own families in the ways of the Lord. We cannot, for our children's sakes, buy in to the current attitude that each of us must "tolerate" the actions, behaviors and attitudes of others, regardless of what they might be. Where there is something wrong, God calls us to point it out.

∽

Planned Parenthood continued to be a thorn in pro-life efforts. I had grown very uneasy with ALL's advocacy of educational programs often described as "chastity education." My discomfort arose from a growing awareness: if parents were indeed the primary educators of their children in matters of faith and morals, then there was no program, regardless of how well-meaning it might be, that we could support if parents were not the main focus. In the vast majority of chastity education materials, for example, the programs were classroom-oriented, and did not focus on parental authority.

Again, it was that nagging memory of the battle I waged at North Stafford High School when Hugh, Cathy and Christy attended classes that urged me to act. The Planned Parenthood folks in Virginia tried to introduce a "Family Life" program into the state's schools. Some of the parents asked me to review the programs that were being considered for use at North Stafford High. In the end, we got more than 150 parents to show up at a school board meeting. We had people pouring into the halls and onto the lawn. Nobody in Stafford County had ever seen so much activity over a "school program."

Because so many parents were concerned over the welfare of their children, the school board backed off and we kept the program out.

When we began to review "chastity" programs in 1995, the memory came back to me, and I called upon our policy staff to discuss it. We had to make a statement and it had better be a good one.

We came to the conclusion that we had to support parental authority. Many of our friends were convinced that chastity

Christy
Brown

education programs were better than Planned Parenthood programs, sort of a "lesser of two evils" argument. But our serious evaluation of the matter convinced us that the proper response is removing all such programs from educational systems, not replacing the bad programs with less offensive ones. Since God entrusts parents to teach their children, then we should tell parents how to teach their children about sexual matters. The parents of North Stafford, during that crucial debate, affirmed my belief that if you want to help parents do a good job with their kids, then all you have to do is help them.

~

The year 1995 also ushered into the Brown family's world our third grandchild, a lovely little baby girl.

Pope John Paul II's encyclical, with its lessons on family life, reiterated for me the miraculous value of every single child—each a gift from God's loving hand. Of all the remarkable things God has done in my life, the most wondrous gifts He has bestowed on me are my husband, my children and my grandchildren.

Obviously grandchildren are a bonus and a tribute to God's glory, His gift of procreation, and His everlasting love for all mankind. In them, as in every one of His children, I can clearly see the reality of God's promise that He loves us more than we can know, and that He will be with each of us always.

Chapter Twenty-two

Infanticide?

1996

But the wise shall shine brightly like the splendor of the firmament, and those who lead the many to justice shall be like the stars forever.

—Daniel 12:3

When I first began volunteering in the pro-life movement in 1969, I never thought that a day would come when I would have to tell anyone a tale like the one that follows.

It is a story about deceptive rhetoric. It is a chilling account of infanticide, which had been given a new name: partial-birth abortion.

From the very beginning, Dr. Bernard Nathanson was quick to point out that infanticide is not abortion. During the initial meeting when new legislation that sought to regulate this "surgical procedure" was unveiled, Dr. Nathanson was impassioned. I distinctly recall his words: "If you do this, you will gravely damage the credibility of the pro-life movement. This procedure involves killing a nearly born infant. It must not be called abortion."

The act is infanticide because the baby is in the birth canal when the act of killing is done. When this act takes place, the baby is turned around so that his feet enter the birth canal first. When the child has been nearly delivered, the surgeon kills the baby by spearing his skull with a pair of scissors. This is infanticide. It is not abortion.

But the strategists in charge at the meeting were undeterred by Nathanson's cautionary note, and their plan moved forward. Ignoring the facts, they claimed that the focus had to be on the shock value of those now famous drawings of nearly-born babies with scissors protruding from their skulls. I had to speak up and express my dismay. But, when I raised my hand, the chairperson said, "This is not going to be debated. Our decision has been made."

Don't get me wrong. The "procedure" is horrific, and it is murder. It is infanticide. It is not abortion. So, why did most groups focus almost exclusively on this act of infanticide, call it abortion, and raise the question during an election year? I wasn't the only one wondering about this.

More and more Americans who are not involved in the pro-life movement began to ask me questions. They asked them in letters to the editor, during call-in radio shows, and on the phone. I cannot believe they were not asking others, too. But maybe I was the only one who would give them a straight answer.

The questions went like this: "Is there such a thing as a particularly bad abortion? Could it be that the millions of real abortions done each year by chemical, device and instrument are somehow less awful than partial-birth abortion? Why would pro-lifers focus on this particular procedure when three others exist that kill babies who are at the very same gestational age but remain totally within the womb during the killing? Don't they know that a hysterotomy abortion kills the late-term child in utero or that an injection into the heart of the late-term child in utero kills her? And has it occurred to them that saline solution placed in the womb will burn the late-term baby to death? So why wouldn't pro-lifers oppose all late-term abortion methods?"

When I had to answer these questions, it sounded so hollow to explain that some of my fellow pro-lifers really believed that these "abortions" yielded the kind of tissue and organs that, once harvested from the dead baby, were in greatest demand in the research community. Everyone knew that was false. The use of fetal tissue and cells in research was focused on the youngest babies, and those aborted during the first trimester were most in demand. So I would usually tell those who questioned me that I had no explanation for any of this. It was clear to me that the whole so-called partial-birth abortion scenario was a sham.

At one point, Dr. Nathanson said to me, "You and I are the black sheep no one wishes to invite to dinner." And he was right. But, being a woman of strong faith in God and common sense, I ask you: why betray the babies? What price are politicians and political operatives willing to pay to "win"?

The result of this debacle was that the nation's attention was focused on a clear act of infanticide, redefined as abortion.

This situation caused me great agony. My heart was broken and my mind was totally befuddled. People who once respected me because I would not cave in verbally accosted me. I had seen all these years of struggle to focus attention on the dignity of the human being evaporate because some believed that a Republican majority was more important that standing for the laws of God. It was so disheartening to me that I had to tell my husband and children that, were it not for my confidence in the power of God, I would have tossed in the towel. After all, I had not spent nearly 30 years of my life in a movement to see this kind of charade played out in public view.

But my husband wisely retorted one day, "Get a grip and take your own advice. Trust God and get to work."

~

So while eyes were focused on one type of killing, the pro-death crowd was busy planning new and better ways to kill.

Clinton's Food and Drug Administration held public hearings on the use of mega-doses of birth control pills as "emergency contraception" or "morning-after" pills. The vast majority of testimony was in favor of the four-pill regimen, and subsequently the FDA found no reason to oppose it. The FDA quietly held these hearings, not because pharmaceutical companies requested them, but because the pro-abortion cartel demanded them. Since the FDA is part of that cartel, not one word has been uttered regarding the health risks these pills pose to women, nor the fact that these pills kill babies. In fact, when charges were made that in fact these pills do kill babies, the FDA denied the charge.

I testified on the chemical effects of these compounds on the baby. My daughter Cathy spoke on the severe health risks to women. Representatives of Pharmacists for Life International did a remarkable job talking about protection of conscience and the proper role of the pharmacist. We called on hundreds of physicians to submit written statements, and we sought the same from pro-lifers. The FDA was overwhelmed with mail, but they decided in favor of the abortionists anyway.

No other pro-life groups testified at this hearing—or even acknowledged the fight.

~

The Planned Parenthood Federation of America boldly discussed their plans to use RU-486 (also known as mifepristone) to abort early pregnancy. They were inspired by the Clinton Administration's support for abortion drugs and by the FDA's approval of a clinical trial process for testing the drug.

We countered with massive letter-writing campaigns, and kept the pressure on through the clinical trial process. We sought testimony from women who had been harmed by the drug and kept close tabs on those who had suffered severely and the few who had died. However, the FDA was deaf to our demands and so were members of Congress.

～

Planned Parenthood and its allies were marketing methotrexate, a drug the FDA previously approved for use as a cancer treatment, as another type of chemical abortion. This is called an "off label" use of an approved drug. In this case the drug had received FDA approval as a cancer treatment, not as an abortion agent. Methotrexate is highly toxic, and when combined with misoprostol, will kill babies during their first eight weeks of life. The abortion proponents never discuss the dangerous aspects of methotrexate, even though the drug firm that manufactures it, Searle, warns of such dangers and specifically notes that it should never be given to pregnant women.

Once again, American Life League and Pharmacists for Life International opposed this tragic practice, but nearly all our fellow pro-life groups remained eerily silent.

～

The year 1996 ushered in a disgusting twist in the in vitro fertilization trade. Labs touted the use of quality control standards so that only "acceptable" human embryos would be considered for implantation in the mother's womb. An embryonic baby would be tested before being placed in the womb, and if the baby failed the quality test, he would be discarded or used for research and experimentation. Most parents seeking such technological reproductive treatments do not know that some of their children will be destroyed.

These labs also proposed using "spare embryos" for specific research studies that would result in the death of the "extras." The embryo, by being viewed as a non-person, became a product. The rejected products could then be treated as trash. With this deplorable state of affairs, pro-lifers had no unified chorus of opposition but only an occasional "Johnny one-note" comment.

We were so concerned about this disturbing turn of events that we sponsored a conference to explore the ethical issues involved in fetal tissue and human embryo research. It paved the way for the formation of the American Bioethics Advisory Commission in 1997. During that conference Dr. Bernard Nathanson gave chilling testimony about how he had come to recognize, through his professional study of human embryology, that in fact a human being is present at conception. This was one reason why he eventually had to stop doing abortions. Ultimately he became a pro-life leader and later a convert to Catholicism.

Several attorneys spoke about the lack of legal protection the embryonic children have, and how loose in vitro clinics are with the facts when they reel in clients to the tune of thousands of dollars per "treatment." We also learned that money was the bottom line for these clinics, and not helping infertile couples.

It turned out to be a turning point for us at American Life League, because we had simply never considered the fact that so many babies were dying in these labs. We knew that we could not be silent. We published many articles helping our fellow pro-lifers see what we had finally seen. This was a chilling time for me because for all these years I had gone around thinking that in vitro fertilization had little to do with pro-life concerns. I was wrong.

$$\sim$$

At the urging of our board of directors, American Life League launched a campaign against American Home Products. This corporation is the parent company of Wyeth-Ayerst, the pharmaceutical firm manufacturing Norplant, an abortive implant that also caused major health problems to women. We purchased a small amount of stock in the company so that we, as stockholders, could issue a pro-life resolution for the annual shareholders' report and meeting. We also invited all the major pro-life groups to join us in a public protest at the shareholders' meeting in March of 1996. None of them accepted our invitation.

But it did not matter because the press had a field day with this project, calling me the "captain of the fertility police." My response was quite simple: "I am pro-woman and pro-child. If a woman is committed to using a birth control implant, surgically inserted into her arm, she should be aware at the outset that she may go blind, she may become sterile, or she may even die. She should understand that her body will still produce eggs; and if these eggs are fertilized, new human lives begin—human beings who will die because of the chemical assault perpetrated by Norplant. Women should not be used as human guinea pigs. Women are not stupid. Women are not playthings for men. Women need to know the facts so that any decision they make is fully informed."

Each time we got involved in one of these battles, whether alone or with others, personhood became a topic for news media interviews. As a result, personhood received wide media attention. Sure, they called me a fanatic, a zealot, and a hard-core pro-lifer. But that's okay. We got the message out there.

~

When the 1996 elections finally took place, the proof of my admonition was clear. Clinton was the hero, winning handily over the squishy Republican candidate. Congressional candidates were measured by tolerance, even when it came to abortion. Those calling themselves pro-life sneaked into office simply because they agreed that regulating "infanticide/abortion" was the goal—period.

~

It was also a banner year for our organization. It was exciting to see what God was doing in Stafford. American Life League adopted the work of Life Education and Resource Network, an African-American outreach project that shared our goal of total protection. What a blessing to work with the LEARN team, led by Akua Furlow, with Pastor Johnny Hunter and his multi-talented wife, Pat.

Pastor Hunter's enthusiasm for life spread like wildfire whenever he spoke. It did not hurt that he had won the hearts of my kids by being one of the most inspired public speakers they had ever heard. Christy heard him at one event and all she could say was "Wow, Mom! This guy is terrific."

ALL issued a second pro-life manifesto, "Letting the Pro-Life Light Shine." I invited pro-life leaders from around the nation to come and discuss the manifesto and how we might use it to unify the pro-life grassroots movement. This positive, pro-active campaign had the complete support of many at every level of pro-life leadership.

The initial meeting produced many tremendous ideas and solid plans for the future of pro-life education and activism including a remarkable little list of the "100+ Pro-Life Things You Can Do," by Greg Chesmore. Greg had been vital to our grassroots outreach program and had become an expert on helping local people do a better job of motivating family and friends.

On the heels of this manifesto, we hosted a meeting in California, "A Salute to Principle," and welcomed nearly 2,000 people to a day of education and praise. Once again, we were lighting candles in the darkness and God blessed that effort.

The year 1996 also ushered in the era of the in-house television studio/radio production studio at American Life League. Our supporters agreed with us that we really needed more "ready for prime time" programming and news information. Thus the studio was built.

It gave us the edge, not only with the press, but also in training our staff, the leaders of our associate groups, and others in how to effectively communicate our message with media.

For me, this was the best news of the year. For just like the challenge of cooking a Thanksgiving dinner for 40 people, all you have to do with these pro-life projects is plan them out, and then do the work. When you bake a turkey, maybe the gravy will be lumpy, but it will work. By the same token, maybe the proj-

Cathy receives her diploma upon graduation from George Mason University.

ect does not go as smoothly as we thought it would. But trying and doing the best we can do is what matters.

~

Things on the home front took on new and thrilling dimensions. We had another grandchild in our midst. She was as cute as her sister, and has made her parents, Hugh and Ann, proud.

Cathy graduated from George Mason University and immediately took a full-time position at American Life League. She exemplifies, to each of us in the family, a remarkable kind of courage and inner strength. She has grown in her faith, her confidence and her abilities to cope with adversity.

Christy graduated from New York University Tisch School of Art, and after a brief visit home, moved on with her life.

Chapter Twenty-three

To Imitate Christ: Drawing the Line

1997

*I speak my thanks earnestly to the
Lord, and in the midst of the throng
I will praise him.*

—*Psalm 109:30*

If ever there was a year of living dangerously in the pro-life movement, this was that year. Here we were in the throes of daily attacks on the dignity of the human person, and nary a reporter could be found who would blow the whistle on the bloodthirsty in our midst.

It has often been my suspicion that the media was really ambivalent about abortion and euthanasia. But during 1997 I learned that the bottom-line motive for most of them was not the bias I had suspected, but was something far more deadly.

When my children were growing up, they were constantly in the midst of one controversy or another, caused either by their mom or dad. To suggest that there was never a dull moment around my home would be an understatement. We often pined for a silent phone, or at least, fewer calls than we were accustomed to receiving from the media. After all, when those children became teenagers, there was a premium on phone calls.

When they were young, I was interviewed with them either listening or sitting quietly in the room. More often than not, when the interview would be printed or aired, we could barely recognize it. There were misquotes, or the editor would excerpt five words from a 60-minute session, and frequently take me out of context. Each of my children had a built-in knack for asking the same question: "Mom, what happened with your interview? Why did they quote you this way? You did not even say this."

Then I would give my spiel. This was based on my view, at the time, that there was a built-in dislike for the pro-life movement. But I never knew exactly why. However, during 1997, as Jack Kevorkian began receiving loads of attention, and human cloning became a topic of wide discussion, I began to see the real media agenda. It hinged on one specific thing: personal autonomy divorced from God.

When columnist Nat Hentoff wrote about Kevorkian, he said that Derek Humphry, founder of the Hemlock Society, once told him "The doors began to open for me and my ideas once a wonderful thing happened—*Roe v. Wade*." Humphry was the founder of the pro-euthanasia Hemlock Society, and had helped his first wife kill herself. So, what Humphry had to say about *Roe v. Wade* not only made sense but was a chilling indictment of our nation and the Supreme Court. What is the basis for a mother's so-called "right" to kill her child? A "right to privacy." Euthanasia proponents base their campaign on a "right to privacy," which translates either into a right to kill (direct euthanasia) or the right to expect someone else to do the killing (assisted suicide).

If you were to review the many articles written about Jack Kevorkian's "suicide machine," there is a common thread: the compassionate thing to do was to kill the sufferer. Report after report resulted in the same bottom line—the victim did not want to suffer and was better off dead. Remember that nurse in the emergency room where my dad was hanging on by a thread? Had I not been there, my dad would have died before his time. Maybe that nurse thought Daddy was a nuisance. Maybe that nurse believed that the hospital beds should be reserved for younger patients. All too often, we hear stories about people who were intentionally killed "for their own good." Kevorkian brought out a side of the media that I wish I had never seen.

Imagine that, in my dad's case, the attending physician had said the cost of caring for my father was immense, and that we, his family, had better uses for the money than providing 24-hour care to a man who was probably going to die anyway. I would have blown my cork.

In my mom's case, Kevorkian would have trotted out his trusty machine, explained to Mom that his way was the best way, and made every effort in his deadly campaign of compassion to convince her that life was over and death was really the way to go. I have learned, especially from dealing with my own mother and father, that when someone is ill and feeling bad about life, those who surround them can make an enormous difference in their will to live. Encouragement, love and time can be the best medicine you can give a loved one who is ill or in a great deal of pain. But if you are unwilling to spend yourself on your loved one, then Kevorkian's solutions can appear very appealing.

My mother often said, "I do not want to be a burden on your father or on you, Judie." I always responded by saying, "Mama, being with you is not a burden. I love you and only wish I could make you better." That was all she needed to hear, and her sadness would soon be overcome by discussions of happy times or current events.

But what if I had said, "Mom, this is really a drag. Why can't somebody do something to help you so I can go home." Emotions being what they are, such a remark could have pushed Mom into depression, which is the state Kevorkian's victims were in when he pranced into their lives with his trusty little killing machine. Some 120 people died because nobody cared enough to help them live, but chose to help them die instead.

The media never made that clear to anyone. And this is why I took it so personally. My own mother and father, in different sets of circumstances, could have been "Kevorkianed."

This is exactly where our society has arrived, following 30 years of decriminalized abortion. Life is cheap and we are told daily that it is right and good to eliminate problems—even if they are human beings.

I wonder why the media never tells us that there is no such thing as "uncontrollable pain." There are physicians who are uneducated about administering pain control in a way that is not harmful to the patient. One study makes the point that when untreated pain persists, patients state a desire for suicide; when pain is treated, suicide is no longer a goal.

No one can say that a particular patient has "six months to live" or a "few months to live." Doctors have all had patients who had only "days to live," and the patients lived for years.

Giving doctors the right to kill is not about giving patients the right to die; it is about destroying the trust between patient and physician. It is about personal autonomy divorced from God. The majority of the so-called media experts are marketing a lie.

~

During this same year, President Clinton appointed his own group of scientists to study the latest scientific advances in human embryo research and human cloning. It was called the National Bioethics Advisory Commission. The NBAC was composed of men and women with an agenda, and not one of them was even remotely pro-life.

American Life League had to enter this debate and be a positive voice in defense of life. Through our American Bioethics Advisory Commission, we recruited attorneys, scientists and others who had the credibility needed to challenge the position that human cloning would benefit mankind and provide therapeutic treatments for deadly diseases. The pro-cloning poppycock now had an antidote. The media was willing to give at least a slight mention to those who do not agree that human beings should be copied like papers in a Xerox machine.

~

I spent hours wondering why Catholics were so ambivalent about abortion and contraception. Here we were, members of a Church that espoused the fullness of truth as the foundation of its existence, and there were hordes of Catholic people who could see no sin in the practices. One poll found that only 36 percent of Catholics were strongly opposed to abortion, and more than 70 percent favored birth control practices. What in the world was going on? Why wasn't the truth of Church teaching reaching all these Catholics?

I realized, of course, that many Catholics who are also prestigious public figures, like Congressman Chris Smith, set a tone that confuses Catholics. Smith had often said, for example, that his drive to remove funding for abortion from foreign aid bills did not mean that he was opposed to family planning.

One cannot blame congressmen. How can a Catholic who hears homilies on everything but Church teachings on marriage, family and human sexuality ever understand why it is a sin to practice birth control or to abort a child?

About this time, a letter arrived from the Vatican. It was from Bishop Elio Sgreccia, vice president of the Pontifical Academy for Life. I had been selected to be a corresponding member of the Pontifical Academy, and asked if I would be willing to sign a document pledging my allegiance to the teachings of the Church. Could you imagine my surprise? Here I was, a housewife, mom and granny from Virginia, with an invitation to become part of the most prestigious body of pro-life Catholics in the entire world.

After my initial tears of joy and speechlessness had worn off, I told Paul and called my kids. With the complete support of my family, I wrote Bishop Sgreccia a letter of acceptance and signed the document he had sent to me.

I could not wait to attend my first meeting, and in the interim, I began a practice of making sure that the academy members were kept up to date on the challenges we face in the U.S. pro-life movement.

I made it my business to learn as much as I could about how the academy operates. I found out that this is a group of men and women who address the same problems we face in the American pro-life movement. The members are from all over the world, and their common interest is defending life and focusing people's attention on Catholic teaching relating to human dignity. My first task was to make sure that I sent each of them any pertinent material that would help them deal with the challenges.

My second task was to read the materials they sent me, so that when I attended my first meeting, I would be prepared. The first set of papers I received from the Pontifical Academy office in the Vatican was a whopping 400 pages. Talk about homework!

Paul and I flew to Rome for that initial meeting, complete with papers, notes I had taken, and great expectation. The meeting would last four days and it was to be held in Old Synod Hall. This is a place within the walls of Vatican City, in the building where the Holy Father lives. I was awestruck.

During our meeting we were escorted through a labyrinth of marble staircases and enormous hallways to a room where we

The Pontifical Academy for Life.

met the Holy Father. He shook our hands and spoke a few words with each of us privately. Paul and I were affected beyond words.

During that first meeting there were debates, and some of them were heated—the topic was human cloning. In a gathering of 100 learned people from around the world, there is not going to be total agreement on any fine point. But at the end of the four-day meeting, when the official statement was made, no one dissented. All of the differences were worked out politely, and total agreement was the result.

I cannot tell you how much I look forward to these annual meetings. I feel a sense of comradeship with all of the members because the common thread that brings us together is total fidelity to the magisterium of the Church. When a group is glued together with that sense of steadfastness, the results of any meeting are bound to be life-affirming and good for the pro-life effort worldwide.

Each time the academy meets we are privileged to visit with Pope John Paul II. He speaks to the entire group during each session. On most occasions, he also individually blesses us and shares a word or two with us. His face radiates overwhelming love and it is extremely difficult for me to speak. I am so overwhelmed as I kneel to kiss his ring and ask his blessing on our work and on all those who support our work.

Pope John Paul II assures me of his prayers for our pro-life work.

Most Catholics only dream of meeting the pope. Yet I have been blessed to be in the presence of Christ's personal representative on earth, not once, but many times. How fortunate I have been!

~

There's never a dull moment at American Life League — just ask the people who work there. It has been said that if you put me in a closet with nothing but a piece of paper and a pencil, I would create five new projects a day.

For example, ALL got involved in battles over human embryo experimentation, domestic and international family planning funding, and a new proposal in Congress that would require health insurance companies to pay for contraceptives, most of which are really early abortion chemicals and devices. It was clear to me that our role in the pro-life movement was to carefully pick the battles where an unwavering pro-life voice was needed.

When it came to the federal government dictating that health insurance companies must pay for birth control, our position was that pregnancy is a very healthy state of being, not a disease. We prepared talking papers, news releases, fact sheets for congressmen and outlines for grassroots people to use in educating others about the absurdity of the argument. I put the whole office to work on this project and asked for help from Pharmacists for Life International and several doctors and health care professionals in the pro-life movement. We needed to have our act together.

We riled folks at Planned Parenthood, whose research group, the Alan Guttmacher Institute, wrote, "In a vociferous denunciation, Judie Brown of the American Life League said, 'These senators apparently view the possibility of pregnancy as a disease that must be medicated. Why else would a physician write a prescription? The bill ignores the tragic physical, emotional and spiritual side effects of all contraceptives.' Leaders of more mainstream antiabortion and self-described 'pro-family' organizations have yet to be heard from. Whether they can dismiss the proposal so easily remains to be seen."

They were frosted. We had made their lives miserable and brought heated controversy to bear when they thought they could get their bill passed without anyone noticing.

The controversy made it impossible for the bill to even be considered that year, so we won.

∼

I speak my thanks earnestly to the Lord, and in the midst of the throng I will praise him.

—*Psalm 109:30*

Often, faith has required me to speak with one of my children about things that may not necessarily resound sweetly in their ears. But in trying to tell them there was a way God would prefer them to do something, we have been rewarded with three adult children who are amazing in their faith and fortitude in times of crisis.

As Father Gerald Weymes, who knows our family very well, has said, "Judie, the devil is going to try to attack you in any way he can. He will attack your children and your husband because by doing so he knows he is hurting you. In the end, if he can get you to quit your pro-life work because of the evils he has visited upon you or your loved ones, then he will have achieved success."

Father Weymes has no idea how frequently I have thought about those profound words. The devil has been alive and well around our family and must be totally frustrated. Because the harder he attacks, the stronger we get. We have the Lord to thank for that strength.

Chapter Twenty-four

God's Will or
Mine Be Done?

~

1998

*Ever since we heard this we have been praying
for you unceasingly and asking that you may
attain full knowledge of his will through perfect
wisdom and spiritual insight. Then you will lead
a life worthy of the Lord and pleasing to him in
every way. You will multiply good works of every
sort and grow in the knowledge of God. By the
might of his glory you will be endowed with the
strength needed to stand fast, even to endure joy-
fully whatever may come, giving thanks to the
Father for having made you worthy to share the
lot of the saints in light.*

—*Colossians 1:9-12*

From the beginning, 1998 seemed that it would be a year that challenged my capacity to stay the course and fight the pro-life fight. For some inexplicable reason the year began with me doubting the very reasons behind the past 30 years of my pro-life involvement. It seemed as though things were slowly slipping out of my control. The agony this caused me is rather difficult to express, but it boils down to this:

My self-importance and my desire to see immediate results was doing battle with my understanding that only in Christ can anything be valuable, be it in this life or in preparation for the life to come.

It boggled my mind that so few leaders in the movement were willing to stand up and articulate, clearly and courageously, that a human being is a person at conception/fertilization. Why couldn't they pursue goals that did not require them to compromise with exceptions? I kept thinking that, after all these years, surely I should have come up with the perfect solution for this. Why wasn't everybody just using their common sense and listening to me?

The governor of Texas, George W. Bush, was considering a run for the White House. He claimed to be pro-life, but his record said something quite different. He favored exceptions: reasons to protect the direct killing of certain babies. I tried in vain to meet with him. But the pro-life people who did meet with him never tried to change his position, just applauded him for his "pro-life" stand. This was extremely frustrating. What was wrong with these people? Why wouldn't someone stand up and join me in pointing out that the emperor had no clothes—he was a sham?

I wrote an editorial on this matter, and submitted it to several newspapers. A few of them actually printed it. But, boy, did the fur fly. First, David O'Steen of NRLC admonished me, though not by name, to stop focusing on the Bush position and start opposing Al Gore. His favorite theme was that a vote for anyone other than Bush was a vote for abortion.

But he was dead wrong. Bush had not yet formally announced that he was seeking the White House. The Republican convention was still two years away. Didn't anyone have the guts to tell Governor Bush he was wrong and needed to strengthen his position?

Many wonder if I have had second thoughts about opposing President George W. Bush. I have not. It is painfully clear to me that the president does not have the preborn child on his radar screen. I know that the events of September 11, 2001, are a great part of the reason why he is distracted. But clearly, as he contemplated the run for the White House, and during his campaign, there were ample opportunities to educate him on the fine points of personhood. I was repeatedly denied access to him. But those who were invited into the inner circle blew it.

I believe in my heart that President Bush could have strengthened his position if we, as a united pro-life political force, had simply expressed to him the personhood principle and resisted the "Republican pro-life" siren song. Our duty is not to a party. It is not to any human being regardless of his perceived power. It is to a God who sets the rules.

I try to follow St. Paul's instruction in 2 Timothy 4, when he said, "Be careful always to choose the right course; be brave under trials; make the preaching of the Good News your life's work, in thoroughgoing service."

Father John Hardon once warned an audience that our greatest temptation in this pro-life work is to fall prey to gaining "human respect" rather than maintain God's. Father Hardon would quote Christ to make his point: "If anyone is ashamed of me and of my words, of him the Son of Man will be ashamed when he comes in his own glory and in the glory of the Father and the holy angels" (Luke 9:26).

∼

When our pro-life involvement began, and particularly when American Life League began, Paul and I believed that we could, together with others, end abortion in a few short months —or at least within a few years. But we had to admit that we were painfully wrong. We underestimated the power of evil. We had placed far too much confidence in the idea that everybody knew that a baby is a baby at conception, and thus most people would reject abortion and the whole idea would fade away. We had been extremely naive.

Paul and I discussed this at some length, and tried to develop a strategy for helping American Life League survive as an institution with principle and survive beyond our years and for as long as it was needed. We laid out a plan for grooming young people into leadership roles in the movement.

We had tried it before, but each time we had a group of young people in place, they left ALL for a variety of reasons. None remained in 1998.

We faced the undeniable fact that we desperately needed to train a crew of equal faith and talent who would not leave. It was my responsibility to make sure that the organization retained its credibility, its integrity and its growth potential.

We began taking stock of those who came to ALL for employment. Out of the clear blue sky, the greatest people started coming to our front door, looking for a full-time role in pro-life work. The degree of their commitment was unparalleled. This was the first of the two major developments of 1998.

∾

The second began as a simple point of information about a subject that interested me. However, this insignificant query turned into a total miracle. From the moment it began, it became an odyssey for me. My spiritual life, my marriage, my family and all that has ever been part of my life fell under a spiritual microscope.

I had been receiving information from Eternal Life, the organization started by Father John Hardon, S.J. I had always been an avid fan of his speeches and his writings.

Among the many things I had read about Father Hardon was the fact that he advocated something called an Ignatian retreat. He had written an outline for such a retreat and provided the tools by which a person could take this retreat at home and not have to leave for a 30-day period, which is the way an Ignatian retreat is usually conducted. I became overwhelmed with the desire to do this "at home" retreat, but realized that Father Hardon recommended doing it only with a trained Jesuit retreat master. Not knowing if such a trained Jesuit was nearby, I called the offices of Eternal Life in Kentucky and spoke with Bill Smith, the director of the organization. Mr. Smith said that he would discuss the question with Father Hardon and get back to me. Just four days later, Mr. Smith called and said, "Judie, Father Hardon would like to be your retreat master. He would like you to call him."

I could not have imagined that Father Hardon would have the time to do the retreat with me. But he did, and this is where my miracle from God began.

Father Hardon discussed the prerequisites for the retreat: setting aside three hours a day for prayer and reflection, following the outline in the book, writing notes about what was going through my mind so that I could fax them to him for review, and attending daily Mass. Finally, he requested that I call him every day, as his availability dictated, so that we could discuss what I had been praying about, thinking and writing.

I thought about the immense time this was going to take from my "important work" and nearly declined. But then I thought, "Judie, something is out of kilter, and this should be done. There is never going to be a convenient time. Just do it."

I told Father Hardon, before the retreat began, precisely how I felt. He talked to me about the "creatures" in my life, and said that as I proceeded with this retreat, I would learn that only by doing God's will can anyone hope to achieve joy and peace of soul. He said that I had to realize that God did not need me to do anything other than to love Him and surrender everything in my life, every "creature" in my life, to Him.

Thus began my adventure into my own soul. Through the process of the retreat, and with Father Hardon's guidance and the advice of my confessor, every spiritual wound I had inflicted on myself was laid open. I can remember the day I experienced uncontrollable tears for no apparent reason. But when Father Hardon explained to me the weight of past sins and the reality of how even the smallest sin hurts Our Lord and causes Him pain, I knew why I had cried. The tears meant I had finally been brutally honest with myself about my own picayune problems, most of which were self-imposed, and none of which were so important after all. My attitudes indeed needed a spiritual overhaul.

I benefited so much from those 30 days that it would take a book just to relate it all. I learned to endure what Father Hardon called "creatures" —the things that would test me and help me develop patience and charity. I learned to eliminate "creatures" that were a hindrance to my life or caused me unease because they were a source of evil or temptation to evil. I learned to enjoy "creatures" God placed in my life to help me grow. I also learned how to discern these "creatures," one of which was my pride.

As I delved ever deeper into my thoughts, feelings and beliefs, I talked openly with Paul. I found that I had grown closer to American Life League than I was to my own husband. At least that was Paul's perception, and I was astounded. Red flashing lights went on in my head.

I had to reorganize my entire life because I realized those three hours a day I spent in that retreat, plus my time at daily Mass, were not interfering in the slightest with the rest of my duties. In fact, every other aspect of my life was going along smoother than it ever had, and the problems I thought were there were diminished—thus revealing the very minutiae they were. I had been making mountains out of molehills, and then expanding them into complete mountain ranges.

When the retreat was completed I had one final discussion with Father Hardon. I wept as Father Hardon, once again by phone, gave me a papal blessing and explained: "Judie, this retreat is really not over. It will never be over. You must continue to pray it, to study it, to reflect on each aspect St. Ignatius sets forth in the retreat. You must never stop going on retreat in your heart and soul."

It was as if my life was starting all over again, with a new focus and a renewed sense of who I was and what God wanted of me. The problems I had perceived at the first of the year were crystal clear to me now, and it was as if God had handed me a map. All I had to do now was follow it, carefully and with a lot of prayer.

It was clear that I had to move my office out of American Life League and into my house. I needed the time to do what everyone told me I did best in the pro-life movement: write, speak and do interviews. I was not a manager and had to make a clean cut with the perception that I was. It was equally clear that I had to train others to lead the organization, thus freeing my time to be the wife, mother and grandmother I not only yearned to be, but God wanted me to be. And of course, I had to prepare for my departure from the active role of president, leaving the task to those with youth and vigor on their side.

Throughout this period, it was clear to me that God was warning me. I had been troubled but did not know why, and now I did.

Less of Judie and more of Christ had to be the order of things in my life for every single moment of my life.

A prayer written by St. Ignatius has become my morning and evening meditation:

Lord, Jesus Christ,
Receive my freedom,
My memory, my understanding and my entire will.
All that I have and cherish You have given to me.
And so I surrender it all to You to be guided entirely by Your will.
Give me only Your love and Your grace, Lord Jesus,
And I will ask for nothing more. Amen.

I am still growing in Him, and realize now more than I ever have, that without Him I am nothing.

～

When I moved out of my office, my marriage improved, as did a lot of other things in my life. As I packed up my office and moved out of the American Life League building, the entire staff was left wondering whether or not I had gone mad.

I explained to them that I might be the world's worst manager. The day-to-day operations of an organization as big as American Life League requires a real manager. It requires someone with the savvy to solve problems and move groups of people in a given direction to accomplish a specified goal. That is not my area of expertise, I told them. No one was shocked to hear this.

Paul was semi-retired, and had turned his company over to the able leadership of our son. Paul offered to manage the day-to-day operations at American Life League as long as his wife "was not there to foul up the works." When they heard that, the entire staff laughed, and American Life League has become stronger and better ever since. I believe that God never intended for me to "run the show." I was learning all about those "creatures" and beginning to understand why God wanted me at home, and functioning as a pro-lifer who lived her convictions by never again putting her family in second place to her pro-life work.

Because nothing happens by accident, the young people I mentioned began to flower at American Life League. I watched them begin to develop, though in 1998 we had but four of the larger group that was to come. Their talent amazes me. God had chosen each of them.

~

Following on the heels of this personal battle was yet another battle with the government. The Food and Drug Administration approved the marketing of birth control pills known as "morning-after pills" or "emergency contraception." The "morning after" was 72 hours long, and the "emergency" was a baby. The FDA had approved chemical abortion.

We were irate about this. The target audience for these pills was going to be the adolescent population. Planned Parenthood made that fact very clear. But no one bothered to tell the public that these pills had never even been tested on young women. It was like watching the FDA make a public statement that, as far as they were concerned, teens were human guinea pigs. Obviously the FDA would do whatever the pro-aborts wanted, regardless of the health consequences. Our board decided that we should sue the FDA. A proper set of legal arguments was pre-

Above: Dr. Mildred Jefferson
Left: Dr. Philippe Schepens

pared, focusing on the deception, the lack of proper oversight and the obvious victimization of women and pharmacists.

A pharmacist who filled a prescription for the pill, or for this newly approved pill regimen, was cooperating in abortion. We were positive we would find men and women who would jump at the chance to become plaintiffs in our lawsuit.

But such was not the case. Late in 1998 our attorney advised us that we were having no success in finding plaintiffs. Though the facts were clear — the pills aborted — we found no one willing to enter the lawsuit either as a victim or as a pharmacist who had not known that the drug aborts children. We attempted several types of advertising to get people to come forth, but no one responded.

I think there was a psychological factor involved here that we failed to take into account. It was evident that few wanted to admit that they had either used or dispensed something that kills people. Maybe they are ashamed. There could be many more reasons for the silence we experienced, but the fact is the public wanted to believe that taking these pills was a good idea.

I think there is a black shroud that hangs around the entire birth control enterprise. Our failed attempt to find plaintiffs for the lawsuit is just one more proof that too many Americans are easily duped. In the final days of 1998 we decided that our effort had gone far enough, and we dropped the suit. There was no reason to pursue it without a plaintiff as we would have simply been thrown out of court.

∼

We had two more reasons to be thankful for God's timing in 1998. Mildred F. Jefferson, M.D., the former president of the National Right to Life Committee, who had invited me on board in 1976, joined the American Life League board of directors in 1998. Dr. Jefferson has always been one of the most dynamic, articulate and sought-after speakers in the history of this movement.

Philippe Schepens, M.D., one of the founders of the World Federation of Doctors Who Respect Human Life and a board member of the Pontifical Academy for Life, joined our board during this same period.

~

    I became convinced in 1998 that "letting go and letting God" is the only way one can possibly live a life for God. As the days progressed after the retreat with Father Hardon, it became evident to me that when we trust God, He makes life amazingly simple. I did not say "easy," but simple. He never leaves our side and He never lets us fail. He only expects us to totally surrender all to Him.

Chapter Twenty-five

The Grand Puzzle

1999

Trust in the Lord with all your heart,
on your own intelligence rely not;
In all your ways be mindful of him,
and he will make straight your paths.
                                    —Proverbs 3:5

I wish to dedicate this chapter to Hugh Richard Brown II, my husband's eldest brother. He passed away a couple of years earlier but his memory is as real as if he were here. Throughout his life Dick, as he was called, inspired the best in others. During his funeral Mass, the priest gave a powerful homily and spoke of Dick with a sentiment that resounds in my heart and soul even now.

The priest spoke of the enormous puzzle that God has created. Man receives the gift of life from God and becomes part of God's master plan for all eternity. In this master plan each human being becomes one piece of the puzzle, with a specific function God has assigned to him. He pointed out that we are often confused because we cannot figure out how we fit in, or precisely what we are going to accomplish in life. In his life, Dick knew that he was not in charge of his world or his destiny, but rather a piece in a puzzle that only God would one day complete. Dick lived his life as a husband, a father and a professor, accepting each day as a gift from God. Dick was an inspiration to others and at peace with his life.

Yes, the priest pointed out, we could fall out of step with the Lord, destroy our opportunity to achieve eternal salvation, and never fulfill the assigned task God has in mind for us. But if we remained faithful, then the Lord would handle the rest. Finally, he expressed to us the need each of us has deep within to trust more in divine providence and less in our own intuition or intelligence. After all, he said, we were not put here to solve the puzzle, but rather to fulfill our role by loving God with our whole hearts, our whole souls, our whole minds and our whole bodies.

Simple, yet extremely wise words. I have often thought about that puzzle, and how it also relates to what we were planning at American Life League in 1999. Never thinking for a moment that I knew what the outcome might be, I set out that year to add young people to the staff, and to train them to be leaders for God, for life and for the building up of the civilization of love.

~

We adopted a careful plan to teach the younger generation of pro-lifers how to be articulate defenders of all God's innocents. The Lord was the master planner, for it was He who carefully, and with perfect timing, brought a group of young men and women to our staff who fit the bill.

One of the key elements required to foster leadership is planting the seeds of truth and helping others learn how to say what needs to be said in a convincing but loving way. I am often reminded of the profound words found in Isaiah 41:10: "Fear not, I am with you; be not dismayed; I am your God. I will strengthen you, and help you, and uphold you with my right hand of justice."

With that in mind, I launched a pro-life philosophy class for these aspiring leaders. I wanted them to know what they were talking about, and I wanted them to ask any question that came to their minds. I wanted them to challenge every policy statement we had so that in learning the facts, they would also quash every doubt they had.

Our greatest concern must be about restoring protection to the little ones and making certain that our actions will have lasting meaning.

~

What happened at American Life League in 1999 is a testimony to the positive results that occur when one surrenders everything to God.

In prayer I had asked for the docility to be open to what the Lord wanted of me, to the point of being willing to remove myself from the office. The Lord blessed that prayer by bringing faith-filled, intelligent young men and women who could be trained for the tasks that lie ahead.

Quite frankly, at 55 years of age, and after nearly 20 years at the helm of American Life League, it was time to start training my successor.

The result of my 1998 conversion to surrender (*Not my will, but Thine*) showed me that when we sincerely ask God to take everything rather than telling Him what He can have, He does. I no longer thought that the pro-life world was mine to lead.

Every corporate leader in the world has a responsibility to look toward the future. We do not know what it holds in store, but we should prepare others for leadership. The nature of our message required young men and women as its conduit. No student is really going to be as motivated when hearing a grand-mother talk about chastity and abstinence. But the message may sink in if delivered by someone who is young. If the presenter is appealing and well-versed, and totally dedicated to Christ as well, how can you refuse to listen?

∼

This brings me to one more 1999 revelation. It had never really occurred to me that the members of the generation born after 1973 are survivors of *Roe* and *Doe*. They are the people who made it—one-third of their generation did not. And it is this cry to listen up and pay attention that they weave so effectively into their speeches. They tell the audience: "I take abortion personally. One-third of my generation, one-third of your generation, is gone."

Just imagine knowing that one-third of your classmates are dead; one-third of the people in the youth choir in your church are dead, even the husband or wife God has chosen for you is dead.

This is a powerful message that is best delivered by the survivors themselves. The message receives resounding applause and leads many to become active in pro-life work.

Left: Rock for Life brings its message to Planned Parenthood (top) and the National Mall in Washington (bottom).

Right: Crossroads teams walk coast to coast on behalf of the babies. Steve Sanborn (far right) launced Crossroads in 1995.

∽

In 1999 American Life League's board of directors launched a conversion campaign aimed at Bill Gates and his wife, Melinda. Gates, the richest man in the world, is also a big supporter of population control programs.

Paul Brown had read extensively on Gates' attempts at philanthropy, and fashioned a campaign around two critical points:

First, the programs Gates was funding were to be called "population elimination" rather than "population control," because their goal was to eliminate the babies of the poor before those babies were born. Paul and I debated this term for a long time, but he won.

Second, Gates is no dummy and is the perfect specimen of a computer geek. To get his attention, we designed a web site just for him. We wanted to goad his best friends into being curious enough to go there and take a look. We fashioned the web site, and the newspaper ads that followed, around the theme, "Twelve Easy Lessons for Bill Gates." If you are as curious as we hoped Bill would be, you can see the site at http://www.all.org/gates/index.htm.

We placed 12 specific messages on the site with loads of links to articles and research supporting the facts. The bottom line was that the world would never be overpopulated. The developed nations in particular are in a lot of trouble. Even the U.N. admits that if some countries do not make dramatic changes they will soon be going out of existence.

The 12 messages ran in local newspapers around Microsoft headquarters just outside Seattle. Those ads generated telephone calls, letters and e-mails.

You would have been surprised at the tenor of a great many of them. None of them had any facts to back up their assertions that the people in the third world were going to overrun the entire planet if they did not stop having babies. In fact, one guy told us that the leading enemy of progress in the world was the pope.

When we responded with charitable comments pointing out the facts, we rarely got a response from these angry zealots. It was a positive and exhilarating campaign.

We got good feedback on this campaign, and are continuing in our efforts to influence Gates' foundation grants. We pray every day for the Gates family, and hope that at some point he sees the facts rather than the illusions created by the population elimination crowd. They are weavers of tall tales designed to appeal to men like Gates, Ted Turner, Warren Buffett and others who have poured millions into programs designed to rid the world of the poor by killing their children.

At a news conference unveiling our series of Bill Gates Ads.

~

During 1999 I gave more than a few interviews about George W. Bush, who insisted that he could favor some abortions and still call himself pro-life.

Many pro-lifers were upset with me. But I had problems with anyone who approved of child killing, regardless of their party. Each time I had the chance to speak out, I did so, regardless of whether I was heckled or applauded. I used that platform to point out that every time pro-lifers support even one exception, they contradict their own principles and agree that some babies are not really persons after all. Since 1973 the number of children killed by abortion has steadily grown. Even though some claim the numbers are going down, we know that chemical abortion is not counted in the totals, nor are all 50 states required to report surgical abortions in a uniform way. What we do know is that in 1999 the Culture of Death had a firm foothold.

I am a zealot, and I am wildly proud of it. I am an enthusiastic supporter for all the babies. I am convinced that every one of them is equally valuable to God. Frankly, if each person who claims to be pro-life would passionately pursue personhood, abortion would be over in the twinkling of an eye.

~

On the home front, Hugh and Ann welcomed their third baby into the world, and their first son. Paul planned a getaway for our 32nd wedding anniversary, but we were unable to go anywhere because I was ill.

Undeterred, Paul planned a second trip for early 2000 and we went away for a few weeks. It is always a pleasure to spend time with Paul, who has lived through all of this with me and has never lost his ability to laugh.

As for those pieces in the puzzle I mentioned earlier, only God knows how and when the puzzle will be complete. But in our case, he put together two pieces that fit so well that our love has cemented these pieces together.

Chapter Twenty-six

Do Not Be Afraid

2000

He said then, "Daniel, do not be afraid: from that first day when you resolved to humble yourself before God, the better to understand, your words have been heard; and your words are the reason why I have come."

—Daniel 10:12

After years of trying to obtain a legitimate voice at the United Nations, American Life League finally won official status as a recognized non-governmental organization—an NGO, in U.N. lingo. We decided that our World Life League division should gather volunteers to work with Bob Sassone, a member of our board, on making that voice heard in effective ways. Bob, author of the *Handbook on Population*, had already built a rapport with several policy analysts at the U.N. and many of the international delegates. Because of his work, more people are learning how to better articulate the facts in areas of population density, food supply and the like.

Bob had done such a masterful job for us in Beijing that it seemed only right that he should make strategic decisions for us at the U.N. when we finally gained our NGO status.

People like Bill Gates are influenced, to a large degree, by the propaganda that spews forth from the United Nations. But as Bob has made clear to many, when the facts are revealed, policy changes and population projections based on truth will be published, rather than population elimination propaganda. Planned Parenthood does not have to be the piper playing the tune; prolifers can replace them. We are having the babies, we are spreading the truth, and we are on God's side.

Mayor Lito Atienza dedicates memorial to the unborn in the Philippines.

~

I have to say a word in this chapter about death, dying and my thoughts on what is occurring in the culture. It has always amazed me that responsible adults seem so ready to take steps that will prematurely end the lives of those they claim to love and care about.

It is far too easy to ask for the death of a loved one for reasons that are anything but honorable and loving. For example, I spent hours drawing attention to the plight of Hugh Finn, a man from my home state of Virginia. He was pronounced "brain dead" by some doctors, but declared comatose by others. His parents said he was aware of his surroundings, but his wife's attorneys, who wanted to remove the feeding tube that provided him with nourishment, described him as a vegetable.

In the end, Hugh Finn was killed under protection of a judicial order that concurred with the diagnosis that Hugh Finn's life should be over. But he was not a vegetable. He was a human being who was in a coma, and only God knew when the time would be appropriate for Hugh Finn's life to end.

What about the patients in hospitals who are pronounced "terminal"? My dad was described that way twice. We were told

Joining with others to demand ethical treatment for nursing home patient Hugh Finn.

that "extraordinary measures" should not be used. Was I to believe that a simple breathing tube was "extraordinary"? Daddy lived another year and a half and he participated in my son's wedding. What if I had gone along with the medical advice?

In my view, no human being should be at risk of losing his life because somebody has declared that he is dead enough to take his organs. Nobody should be ushered out of life because he is too ill to recover.

This is why I urge people, at every opportunity, to make sure that they have signed a "loving will" or a similar document. I also counsel people to never sign an organ donor card. I have nothing against organ donation. It is a charitable and laudable act. But I do have a problem when a living person becomes a dead person because his heart was taken before he had expired.

◆

It disturbs me that the media seems all-too-ready to twist the words of anyone who speaks the truth, even if that person is Pope John Paul II. When the Holy Father delivered an address to transplant surgeons, I hoped the media would really examine the term "brain death." Innocent people can be killed if the diagnosis of "brain death" coincides with an urgent need for a fresh organ or with a request from a family member to be "relieved of the agony."

However, the media aligned the pope with the merchants of death by misquoting and misrepresenting what he had said. It seems that whenever one of us who is on God's side attempts to correct a reporting error in the media, the correction is rarely made. As a result, great damage is done—damage that can linger for years.

◆

The year 2000 brought another presidential election. Americans had to choose between Al Gore, a near clone of Bill Clinton, and George W. Bush, the son of a previous resident of the White House.

When I looked at all the statistics from those elections, the one thing that really blew me away was that the majority of Catholics in our country voted for Gore.

In my mind, this confirms what I suspected for years. We have a crisis in the nation that is not being addressed effectively from the pulpit. This crisis centers around the word "responsibility."

Here is how my Responsibility 101 lesson goes.

Human beings are special, and each one of us is unique—an unrepeatable expression of God's love. When it comes to valuing the human person, the game of politics should not be played – ever. Abortion is not a "political issue."

Look at a newborn baby. Can't you see in that beautiful child the amazing miracle of God's love? Does that baby look like an issue to you? Does she look like a "choice?" Does she look like a Democrat or a Republican?

The correct answer is that it's a baby—anybody can see that. So why in the world should it be any different for the baby who is growing but not yet born?

When you really think about that baby, one thing is perfectly clear: the act of abortion is not a political issue. It is a matter of life and death. Therefore, choice for or against abortion is a choice between good and evil, not between political parties.

If enough Christians were committed in their pro-life vocation, then America would not be slaughtering millions of her own citizens every year.

So why are Catholics, people who have been blessed with the teachings of our Church, so apathetic about their pro-life vocation? Why do they vote for men and women who support killing people by abortion?

A textbook example unfolded in Massachusetts, where Phil Lawler ran for the Senate against Ted Kennedy in 2000. Lawler is a good man, well-known to Catholics as the editor of *The Catholic World Report*. He has been involved in Massachusetts politics for some time. But in this election in Massachusetts, a very Catholic state, he received less than two percent of the Catholic vote. What happened?

Lawler summed it up this way: "Are most American Catholics actively opposed to the Church's teachings on the dignity of human life, are they indifferent, or are they simply not paying attention? In any case, the Catholic Church has failed to sway the political opinions of her own faithful. My excursion into secular politics leaves me more convinced than ever that we cannot expect reform in society at-large until we achieve reform within our Church."

When the majority of Catholics and other people of good will understand the gravity of what abortion does to a person, this nation will begin the slow process of healing and turning back to God. The fact is you cannot be pro-life in a faith vacuum. If you do not believe that God is the author of life, then clearly life is expendable. If you do not believe that there is sin, and that abortion could land your soul in Hell, then anything goes.

When America starts hearing this message from the pulpit regularly and consistently, grace is going to pour forth on the people of this nation in ways we cannot even imagine.

Maybe you'd like to get the ball rolling in your own Church right now. If your pastor has rarely spoken about the dignity of the human being, or about abortion, then you should offer to help him out. Offer to be his hands and his feet and to provide anything you can to help him prepare sermons that will share the Gospel of Life with his flock.

By attempting to be part of a solution to a huge problem, I think you can win him over. It has worked for me. My own children have done things that provide encouragement to priests. Hugh sits on the board of a local crisis pregnancy center. He sacrifices his time, and others in his parish are

Hugh Brown carries on our family tradition of pro-life work.

motivated to do likewise. Cathy has willingly taken time to help educate the youth groups in her parish. She saw a need and volunteered to help fill it.

It is always better to be the candle lighting the way than to be the one who snuffs it out and then screams about the fact that he cannot see. We must never fear what lies ahead. It takes total trust in God and a sincere desire to belong totally to Him.

⁓

The crowning joy of 2000 was a bold new idea. Paul proposed that we build a pro-life institute, which would be called the Culture of Life Campus. This vision included a new administration building for American Life League, a media-training center with adjoining classrooms, a bioethics center complete with research lab, a chapel dedicated to Christ the King, a basement containing even more meeting rooms, and a pro-life Hall of Honor. The Hall of Honor would be dedicated to the unsung heroes of our movement.

Distance learning has become so popular that we decided the massive library we have been building since 1979 should become an electronic library for those who wish to do research online. Why not teach the message over the internet? Other organizations do it. Bill Bennett has an entire curriculum for homeschoolers on the internet.

We began a campaign to raise money for the campus in the belief that not only was such a campus needed but also that all things are possible with God.

Through the grace of God, we were able to acquire 139 acres in Stafford County, Virginia, where real estate prices are sky high, for one-fourth of the actual value. The man who represented the 13 owners of this land expressed his pro-life principles to us and made a donation to our work when the deal was closed.

We have sought the will of God and He has shown us, through the events that have taken place, that He is with us. We owe every achievement that we accomplish to Him and Him alone.

Chapter Twenty-seven

Enough Is Enough

~

2001

*I will bless the Lord at all times; his praise
shall be ever in my mouth.*

—Psalm 34:2

Paul and I crossed another threshold early in 2001 because of a seed Our Lady planted deep in our hearts one cold, rainy afternoon in Toledo, Spain. We were visiting a cathedral there as part of a pilgrimage. We entered the cathedral and were ushered to a side altar, which contained a statue of Mary holding a six-month-old infant Jesus. The infant was cupping his mother's chin in his hand, and they were looking at each other with smiles and adoration. We had never seen such expressions depicted on the faces of Mary and the Christ child.

The impression this white marble statue made on us was indelible. As we stood there looking at it, we were both thinking that this image was perfect for pro-life America. When we left the cathedral, we searched Toledo from top to bottom for a photo or picture of some sort to take home. In all our searching we only found one small picture in a guidebook.

In early 2001, we discussed this image with Paul's niece, Theresa, who is a remarkable portrait artist. She agreed to

Left: Our Lady of Life.

Below: Bishop John Yanta at ALL's 2001 conference with me, Fr. Denis O'Brien and Fr. Joseph Howard.

attempt a painting that would reflect the joy she saw—even in that small image in the guidebook.

The result was 4 by 8 foot oil painting that brought tears to the eyes of nearly every member of our staff.

We felt this portrait, "Our Lady of Life," was the perfect image to counteract the evil influences of feminist rhetoric regarding the vocation of motherhood. As we know all too well, motherhood has become a second-class profession in the eyes of millions.

Our Lady of Life, whose portrait was blessed by Bishop Thomas J. Welsh at ALL's 2001 conference in Minneapolis, is American Life League's patroness. A grotto dedicated to Our Lady of Life is a key component in ALL's proposed Campus of Life. When the campus is complete, it is my prayer that the Our Lady of Life Grotto will become a focal point for pro-lifers who come to learn, pray and reflect.

~

Right after the Pontifical Academy for Life meeting in February 2001, Paul and I took a trip down the Amazon River in Brazil. We saw so many examples of God's handiwork in nature, including the river itself. One cannot fathom the tons of earth this river moves on a daily basis. This river is the only way for most residents of the Brazilian state of Amazonia to get around. Even the little children, as young as six, take their canoes to go to school in the morning. The adults take hammock boats to and from the state capital, Manaus, to buy and sell produce, livestock and crafts.

The sights and sounds of the Amazon are beyond words. But it is the people who affected me most. I did not see any feminist protests in the Amazon villages or in the capital. I did not see any abortion mills, though I am sure the death peddlers are hard at work helping the poor by killing their babies. What I did see were smiling faces and kind, caring people. Their children are very important to them, and cherished. No, they do not wear designer clothes. But they wear hearts as big as all outdoors.

Their love of life reminded me of the very reason why some of us persist in the struggle to defend our brothers and sisters in Christ.

If only we, who live in the "developed" West, could learn from our brothers and sisters along the Amazon what is important. It is knowing that we belong to God, and expressing the love that prompted God to create each of us. Man is a sign of His love. Let us strive for the day when each American recognizes that sign and stands ready to defend it against any sort of attack.

Chapter Twenty-eight

Looking Back–
Trial or Triumph?

~

2002

*No test has been sent you that does not
come to all men. Besides, God keeps his
promise. He will not let you be tested
beyond your strength. Along with the test
he will give you a way out of it so that you
may be able to endure it.*

—*1 Corinthians 10:13*

No one knows the depth of another's suffering unless he has walked in the other person's shoes. This is why God asks us to love others as He loves us, not make judgments about what they do or experience or feel. Rushing to judgment usually leads to error —at least that has been my humble experience.

Throughout these pages I have shared with you the agonies and the joys of my life, and have tried to give you a taste of what it means to be pro-life, not in a public, "attend a meeting" kind of way, but in the way we actually live.

One of the most profound messages of the Gospel of Life is that man is called to service. He is called to be in solidarity with his brothers and sisters in Christ. This means that every simple act of kindness toward another, especially when it is difficult to perform, is a pro-life statement. Every such deed is a testimony to our acceptance of Christ's invitation to follow Him, to take the narrow road and to trust in His guiding light. The best way to love is to give, for only in giving love can we ever hope to receive it.

I recall again what Father Gerald Weymes told me: "Judie, the devil is going to try to attack you in any way he can."

What the devil did not take into account was that, through the grace of God and a whole lot of prayers, every single time he attacked one of us, he only made us more committed than ever to Christ the King.

The Browns know how ugly Satan can get. In fact, we renew our dedication to Christ each day because we each know now that the devil never sleeps.

Paul became the target of the evil one's flaming arrows on more than one occasion. As so frequently happens to businessmen, there were times when Paul was faced with choices that could lead to peace or pain. I cannot tell you how often he agonized about clients, personnel and other matters. All too often they were the kinds of decisions that would change lives forever because they had to do with the livelihood of a particular family.

Paul has taught me much about how a business should be run, and he has been a guiding force for how we treat our staff at American Life League. The value a company or charity places on a person is in direct proportion to the relationship those in charge have with the master of us all.

God continues to amaze us with the realization that His gentle caring hand continually rests on each of our lives. As a mother, I am eternally grateful to the Lord for the great blessings He has given us in our children.

The home is the domestic church, according to Pope John Paul II. And each home should radiate that grace that comes with lives lived in a peace that is not of this world.

Each of our family members has faced the worst Satan could have thrown at anyone. After having reflected on these situations for a long time, each of us became, in that hour of trial, another Eleazer.

Perhaps you are not familiar with that amazing Biblical tale, but I would like to share it with you because it might help you when the going gets tough, and the tough need to get going.

In 2 Maccabees 6:18-31, we read about the trial of the prophet Eleazer. He was in trouble with the local authorities and was being forced to eat the flesh of a pig, something that he could not do as a man faithful to the laws of that day. But we are told that those who were in charge of this challenge to Eleazer's faith in God had long been his friends. So they asked him to prepare meat that he could eat according to the law, but then to publicly pretend that he was eating the meat being forced upon him. His reaction to this deceptive idea is worth quoting:

"Such pretense," he said, "does not square with our time of life; many young people would suppose that I at the age of ninety had conformed to the foreigners' way of life, and because I had played this part for the sake of a paltry brief spell of life, might themselves be led astray on my account; I should only bring defilement and disgrace on my old age. Even though for the moment I avoid execution by man, I can never, living or dead, elude the grasp of the Almighty. Therefore if I am man enough to quit this life here and now. I shall prove myself worthy of my old age, and I shall have left the young a noble example of how to make a good death, eagerly and generously, for the venerable and holy laws."

His fair-weather friends who had tried to cajole him into deceptive activity became outraged at this response, turned on him and beat him to death. But as he was dying, Eleazer said he was "glad to suffer, because of the awe which God inspires in me."

Eleazer so loved God that he refused to betray Him. He knew that others would see his deceptive act and be misled, perhaps into sin, if he were to accept and perform the evil act proposed to him. In other words, his virtuous love of God prevented him from falling into Satan's grip even though the temptation to stray from the law of God must have been enormous. After all, Eleazer was a human being just like you and me.

This is the lesson to be learned from the challenges and crises Satan imposes on each of us on our journey to eternal joy with Christ. When we stumble, hell wins. When we stand strong and believe that Christ is ever by our side, heaven wins.

The choice is ours. In the end, that is what abortion and its progeny are all about. The choice is nothing less than heaven or hell.

Left: Father Denis O'Brien, M.M.

Below: Fr. O'Brien with the children at Pastoral Del Amor in Yucatan, Mexico, a home for retarded and terminally ill children which he founded.

It is not easy to follow the straight and narrow; but the enormity of blessings that await those who stay the course make the right choice worth the sacrifice, whatever that may be.

ALI's spiritual director, Father Denis O'Brien, M.M., once said, "When things get difficult, remember the words St. Joan of Arc spoke to the king as he was about to order her execution: 'You have your advisors, and I have mine.' She meant, of course, that you must follow the will of God and never count the cost. Do what is right though the heavens fall." When things got really bad and the devil was particularly antagonistic to me, Father O'Brien would say, "Why worry? God is laughing. Why aren't you?"

Father Denis O'Brien will always live in my memory as someone who never, ever failed to put God first. Therefore, with that in mind, I offer this prayer for you: "May God always give you the inspiration to see what He wants for you. He will never let you down."

$\sim$

Wherever I have come from, I am still going forth. Wherever I have been, I hope I have made a difference. Whatever I have done, it has really been the Lord working through me, since by myself I can do nothing.

Mother Teresa has said that she is nothing but a pencil in the hand of God. Oh, that I might be such an instrument.

I have laid my life before you, but not to draw attention to myself. My only hope has been that by seeing how God has worked through another ordinary person, you will be motivated to turn to God and ask, "Lord, what would you have me do?"

I know that one day the killing will stop. Our Lord is too merciful, and too powerful, for it to be otherwise. But He has chosen to do his work through us, the weak things of the earth. Have we yielded ourselves to His power and purpose as fully as we should? Have we pleaded with Him as earnestly as we should for an end to the slaughter? Have we thanked Him lately for loving us more than we could ever imagine?

I conclude with one of my favorite passages from a layman's version of St. Thomas Aquinas. I think it will encourage you, as much as it does me, every time I read the words:

A Reflection on God from St. Thomas Aquinas

We are not hidden from God by our cowering, nor is our reaching for Him a matter of distance. He is indeed not far from any one of us; rather, He is in us, as He is in every created thing, profoundly, intimately, more present to us than we are to ourselves. Our very being, and the being of everything we have, we are, or we meet is a borrowed thing, as the firelight is a loan from the flames. An instant of separation from God would be instant annihilation, for every moment of our life is nourished from the very life of God, more dependent on that life than an infant in the womb is upon the life of the mother. Our hearts can wander far from God, but God is not far from our hearts for we are more His than our own.

God loves you. Ask for His help. With Him and through Him, victory is assured.

Afterword

The Challenges
We Face

Stem cell research

Stem cell research based on the destruction of embryonic persons received the backhanded support of the White House in 2001. The abortionists are having a field day with a White House preoccupied with "compassionate conservatism." To top it all off, allegations of human cloning efforts being successful in producing "something" made headlines all over the world.

What you may not know is that not much has changed for the babies since Bill Clinton left office. In 1996 Congress prohibited human embryo research using federal funds. The amendment, which American Life League helped draft, states that no Department of Health and Human Services funds can be used to "create a human embryo or embryos for research purposes; or for research in which a human embryo or embryos are destroyed, discarded, or knowingly subjected to risk of injury or death greater than that allowed for research on fetuses in utero." This language was not what we wanted because it did not ban all such research and experimentation regardless of the source of funding. However, because it was being added to a federal appropriations bill, and was not a new law unto itself, it was the only tactic we could take at the time to at least put a halt to our tax dollars being used for human destruction. At least, that is what we naively thought.

What the Clinton Administration did was set the DHHS lawyers to work interpreting the amendment so it did not actually prohibit human embryonic stem cell research. The only way to obtain such stem cells is to kill an embryonic person. I think you should read exactly what those DHHS lawyers said: "human embryonic stem cells are not a human embryo within the statutory definition" because "the cells do not have the capacity to develop into a human being even if transferred to the uterus."

With these words the Clinton Administration ruled that federal funds could be spent to use body parts from embryonic babies as long as those embryonic people were killed in the private sector. The Clinton argument is the very same argument George W. Bush used when he made his statement on the matter on August 9, 2001. In both cases, Clinton and Bush trampled personhood into the ground by drawing the line—not in defense of personhood—but in prohibiting only certain dollars from being used to kill the embryonic person.

Are you confused? Take a look at the Clinton language again, and notice the words not stated. A human embryo is a human being at fertilization. Removing stem cells from a human embryo has the same result as removing the heart of a human adult— immediate death. You cannot live without your heart; the embryonic baby cannot live if her stem cells are removed. The intelligentsia believe that a person is not a person at fertilization, but only a clump of cells with "potential." Thus, in this line of thinking, the destruction of that clump of cells is not immoral.

The act of killing a child who lives in his mom is described as a choice.

The act of killing an embryonic child is described as stem cell research.

The clincher in all this is that the most successful stem cell research, according to scientists themselves, is that which uses stem cells from patients themselves or from the cord blood that remains in the afterbirth when a baby is born. There have been no successes using stem cells from human embryos.

Each time American Life League has testified or commented against such practices, the media has amazed us. They actually listen to us and report precisely what we are saying. They are particularly fascinated by the comments of our American Bioethics Advisory Commission. We praise God for that, and also for the articulate effort that the Catholic bishops have put into this campaign. It is nice to have allies in such battles for the hearts and minds of the citizenry.

Chemical abortions

The abortion industry has upped the ante by focusing more attention on the needs of women to have their freedom of choice expanded so that they can effectively kill their children earlier and with greater efficiency. But again, nobody uses the word "child" or the word "baby" and never the word "mother." It's all about reproductive health care.

The National Abortion Federation is leading the battle to make sure women across the land know that they can get chemical abortion. They launched a major advertising campaign in women's magazines with an emphasis on those publications read by teens. The advertising discussed the value of the RU-486 (mifepristone) plus misoprostol abortion. What is interesting about the ad campaign is the absence of any health warnings, and its failure to point out that the abortion being promoted requires at least two or more visits to a "clinic." Before a woman can receive her chemical abortion pills, she has to agree in writing to a surgical abortion if the chemicals fail. Somehow those facts failed to appear in the NAF ads.

Planned Parenthood and their allies continue to work with the bureaucracy of the Food and Drug Administration to get an "over the counter" agreement on the birth control pill and the morning-after pill. These pro-abortion advocates have assured, in the law, that pharmacists have the right to hand out the morning-after pill abortion kit without a doctor's prescription. Though this poses dangerous health risks, particularly to teens, the project has been most successful, and has inspired Planned Parenthood to move ahead in a national effort.

Human cloning

Human cloning is a subject that is shrouded in half-truth, media hype and colossal ignorance. It is sustained by deep pockets filled with all kinds of money. At American Life League we have had the benefit of advisors like Professor Dianne Irving, a scientist who understands the manner in which the public is being intentionally misled. In addition to her expertise, we have the American Bioethics Advisory Commission to advise us.

As Professor Irving has testified, the creation of the mythical term "pre-embryo" has led to more killing and human destruction than anyone can calculate. Only God knows the extent to which our nation has murdered its future.

In the case of alleged human cloning successes, there is no shred of evidence to support the claim that a human clone has really been produced. We know how frequently these emperors of science manipulate the language. What I have to say to them is quite simple: prove it. In the meantime, we are busy exposing the fact that these emperors have no clothes—and no moral principles either.

Personhood: The Vision

The key to winning the struggles we face in the future, be it opposing stem cell research, human cloning or chemical abortion, is to make certain we do everything we can to focus our attention on the person who exists at conception/fertilization. There is no difference between an adult and the person who is but a single cell. That youngest human being is just smaller and needs time to grow and flourish. God knows what He is doing, and our job is to make sure that everyone recognizes personhood as a fact that cannot be disputed.

American Life League's formula for this cultural turnaround is based on the premise that if someone is exposed to the truth, even though he first rejects it, he will think about it. At that point, his mind will be open to the power of God. Then the miracles can begin. This is why we have so diligently pursued uniting the pro-life movement, issuing the Declaration on Truth and Life, adding divisions to our organization and cultivating associate groups around the world. We have not forgotten academia, where so much of the trouble begins. Our American Bioethics Advisory Commission is designed to counter the evil influence of those who teach our children that right is wrong and wrong is right.

We reach out to people of all ages with our various publications, and the proof that our vision is taking hold is the thriving outreach programs in which our youth divisions are involved. We are constantly bombarded with requests from the younger generation, and God has blessed us with people who unselfishly give of their time.

In God's good time all that we envision for a complete restoration of a civilization of life will come to pass. It has to.

It seems to me that most in our nation sit by in idle apathy, waiting for the next headline. Then far too many of them look to the Dan Rathers or the Bill O'Reillys to tell them what the headlines really mean. Too many in our midst are guided, not by knowledge or faith, but by rhetoric and spin. What a tragedy this is, not only for those who lose their lives by acts of abortion, euthanasia and other practices, but also for those who, in an apparent state of indifference, unwittingly contribute to the mass slaughter by believing what others say about matters of life and death. Very few bother to take the initiative to verify what they hear.

I recall William Saletan's editorial, "The Ethicist's New Clothes." He pointed out, regarding the current cloning craze, that "credentials and committees don't make you ethical. Principles do. Those principles have to make sense. You have to apply them consistently or rethink them if you can't stomach their implications. And the easier you make them, the less they matter."

See the implication in his words? If you do not like your principles, then rethink and modify them. If you do not like to think about abortion as murder, then call it "choice." If you do not want to admit that you are responsible for your own actions, then argue that you have "reproductive rights." This is why America is killing people. Right and wrong are totally subjective.

All ethical principles must be based on the Commandments of God. God's law must be followed if civilization is to survive. Otherwise, chaos will rule. And chaos is ruling. Babies are dying at an alarming rate, and too few are aware of it or even care to know about it.

The antidote to this tragedy is in our vision—opening minds, touching hearts, and with God's help, being a healing force to all those already wounded by the crimes of abortion and euthanasia. We ask you to join us and become part of the new civilization of life—and love.

In Memoriam

~

Father Denis O'Brien, M.M.
Spiritual Director,
American Life League
October 8, 1923 — August 29, 2002

*Fr. O'Brien and
Judie Brown.*

~

The world is a lesser place because Father Denis O'Brien, M.M., has gone to his heavenly reward. But this humble priest touched many with his awesome example of God's gracious love.

Father Denis O'Brien was born in Dallas on October 8, 1923, and entered the seminary in 1941. But when Pearl Harbor was attacked, he quickly volunteered for the Marine Corps.

He served in the Pacific, and often recalled the battle to take Peleliu as the bloodiest and most memorable—1,336 Marines lost their lives and 6,032 were wounded.

He said it was on that battlefield that he felt God's call stronger than before. After he left the military service, he went into God's service by studying at the Maryknoll Seminary in New York.

Father Denis O'Brien went on to be a missionary to the poor, the needy, the terminally ill and the "unwanted" in East Africa and Mexico. Father O'Brien so impressed the leadership of the Mexican bishops' conference that he was appointed respect life director, a job he performed remarkably for 25 years. He trained doctors, taught medical students, spoke to high school and college groups, trained parents, and did it all with a love for human beings and respect for the magisterium of the Church.

In my mind, one of Father O'Brien's greatest accomplishments was his work in Mexico that produced the first ever catechism for retarded children and adults. It was available in Spanish and in English, and made the teaching of basic Catholic truth come alive for retarded children.

Beyond that, Father O'Brien wished to establish a home for retarded and terminally ill children. He wanted a safe haven where abandoned children could be loved. So he put together a team of very special people in Merida, Yucatan, Mexico and established the first Pastoral Del Amor orphanage.

He became the spiritual director of American Life League at its founding in 1979. In fact, he cajoled us into starting ALL because he saw a need for a pro-life organization committed first and foremost to the Catholic Church and her teachings on the dignity of the human person.

When he first encountered cancer 15 years ago, he moved from Mexico back to Dallas where, he said, "the doctors helped me lick the disease." Afterward, he made many trips back to Yucatan, taking the best doctors in America with him to help his children at Pastoral Del Amor.

In Dallas, Father O'Brien embraced and affirmed so many people at St. Pius X Parish. One family wrote this note on his 73rd birthday: "This man comes over to our home as often as his duties permit. He tells our five children to call him 'grampa' knowing they haven't one around. He sometimes brings goodies and teaches the children to bless each other and their parents too! Then he is off to one of his many meetings and ministries. 'No rest for this poor sinner,' he waves as he runs out the door."

Father Denis O'Brien would not approve of this tribute I write on the occasion of his death. He would tell me that he does not want any credit for any of the things he ever did; he wants only to know that God approves. He would remind me that in living our daily lives we are to focus on Christ and never on ourselves. In his final days, he would say that being with the many men and women who helped care for him each day gave him a chance to work on their eternal salvation. And then he smiled. Always the sly one, he knew what he was about—and that was doing God's work.

So many will miss him; so many will pray for the happy repose of his soul. But I have a sneaky feeling that he is going to be interceding for each of us in ways only God will ever know—and that is exactly the way Father Denis O'Brien would like it!

— Judie Brown, president
American Life League

Get your FREE pro-life catalog!

Check out our entire line of popular pro-life T-shirts, no-compromise educational materials, and great-looking posters and bumper stickers! It's all in the ALL Catalog of Pro-Life Resources. We hope our offerings help you and others to think, to see and to work together, embracing God's amazing gift of life! The catalog is free—and so is the phone call. To get your copy, just call toll-free 866-LET-LIVE.

Got a computer? Shop online!

You can find many of the items from the ALL Catalog of Pro-Life Resources at the best pro-life shop on the internet! Use your credit card and our secure server to order the most popular resources from our catalog—and that includes the best-selling ProLifeGear line of apparel from ALL's Rock for Life youth division. Just go to the ALL web site at www.all.org, click on Pro-Life Store, and start filling up your shopping cart!

Judie Brown Report

One of the most widely read pro-life newsletters ever, *The Judie Brown Report* offers a monthly summary of the latest developments in the life-and-death cultural war that divides our nation. Every issue features eight fact-filled pages on topics ranging from Planned Parenthood, to the United Nations, political analysis, and science updates, as well as Judie Brown's monthly commentary and a calendar of upcoming events. *FREE* with a donation of $10 or more to support the work of American Life League.

Call 888-546-2580 or go on-line at www.all.org to make a donation.

Reality Check

Let's face it, when you're a teen trying to sort things out in modern America, you're going to need at least one reality check a month! This monthly pulication of American Life League's youth division reaches out to young people everywhere with the pro-life message. *Reality Check* is a haven where you can meet people who love life as much as you do.

Call 888-546-2580 to subscribe.
Yearly subscription: $12.00

STOPP International's
Ryan Report

A monthly newsletter that is the voice of STOPP, American Life League's division whose purpose is to expose the true nature of Planned Parenthood and document its anti-life, anti-family programs.

Ryan Report subscribers also receive a two-page monthly STOPP Update that gives an in-depth look at timely pro-life issues.

Call 888-546-2580 or go on-line at www.all.org/stopp/support.htm to subscribe. Yearly subscription: $25.00

Free e-mail newsletters

Communiqué

Few contemporary issues create more controversy, more criticism or more cultural currents than the pro-life movement. *Communiqué* provides an easy, accessible way to stay up-to-date on regional, national and worldwide developments that affect the sanctity of life. *Communiqué* is distributed weekly. To subscribe, e-mail jbrown@all.org and ask to be placed on the *Communiqué* list.

Rock for Life Newsletter

The fastest-growing segment of the pro-life movement in America is among teens. They're hungry to hear the truth and quick to understand that a third of their generation has been lost to the Culture of Death. Teens use the Rock for Life newsletter to learn about upcoming events, action opportunities, pro-life music reviews and so much more. Just go to www.rockforlife.org and click on "join our newsletter."

Vine and Branches

Many women and men who struggled for years with the pain of abortion have found healing through ALL's Rachel's Vineyard division. *Vine and Branches* shares news about a ministry that began as a small seed, and through God's power, and the loving service of so many laborers, has continued to bear abundant fruit. To subscribe to *Vine and Branches*, go to www.rachelsvineyard.org and click on "newsletter."

Give a gift for life to ALL!
Get an income for life for you!

With American Life League's Charitable Gift Annuity . . .

. . . you're assured of receiving a guaranteed income for life. And you'll know that your gift to *ALL* will be used to defend all life for years to come.

The benefits of an *ALL* Charitable Gift Annuity:

- A lifetime fixed income at a very attractive rate.
- Immediate and ongoing tax advantages.
- Satisfaction in helping *ALL's* mission to protect life.

For more information about an ALL Charitable Gift Annuity, call Patrick Murphy at 1-888-546-2580.

This program is not available in all states.

Sample rates*	
Age	**Rate**
20	4.80%
30	5.20%
40	5.40%
50	5.70%
60	6.40%
70	7.20%
80	8.90%
90	12.00%
*one life rate	

Where there's a WILL there's a WAY.

Here's how to make sure your love for life lives on.

A memorial gift to *ALL* in your personal will ensures that your love for all innocent human life will be part of the living legacy you leave behind. Your generous remembrance of *ALL* is the best way to make certain that the babies—and your love for them—are never forgotten.

If you'd like more information about how to include *ALL* in your will, call us at 888-546-2580 and ask for our brochure entitled: "Your Will—A lasting reflection of your love."